THE KEY
to a
RICHER LIFE

"Thoughts are like seeds... You reap what you sow!"

Carsten Frölich

BENEDICTE FRÖLICH

THE KEY to a RICHER LIFE

"Thoughts are like seeds... You reap what you sow!"

How to turn Self Help, Personal Growth and Development into a Successful Living

Copyright © 2012 Benedicte Frölich

2. Edition – 1 Printing - Createspace 2015.

Publisher – Three Leaves Publishing

Cover – Benedicte Frölich

Photo - Frank Gormsen

Illustration - Carsten Frölich

http://www.personligsucces.nu

ISBN: 978-87-93015-13-5

Original Danish title:

Nøglen til det rige liv - *Tanker er som såsæd... Du høster hvad du sår!*

~

REVIEWS

~ *Brian Tracy* - Author of "The Power of Self-Confidence"

"This excellent book shows you how to release your potential for happier, more successful living."

~

~ *Kyle Wilson* - Founder of Jim Rohn International and YourSuccessStore.com and author of "52 Lessons I Learned from Jim Rohn and Other Legends I Promoted"

"Is more knowledge the key to success? Working harder? Being around the right people? Well the answer could very well be given in Benedicte Frölich's book *"THE KEY to a RICHER LIFE"*. Ultimately as she so clearly defines, it is up to each of us to work through life's equations and the unique scenarios we are given. Benedicte supplies the road map and a fog light to get you through some of life's challenging issues and helps you then reach your own goals to success."

~

~ *Gerry Robert* - Author of "The Millionaire Mindset"

"If you want to simply exist in the bland zone of mediocrity, then Benedicte's book is not for you. If you want a Millionaire Mindset and live the Richer Life, then it is definitely for you. You will want to go beyond just reading this book. You want to study it and mine the riches that are contained within."

~

~Vic Johnson - Author and founder of AsAManThinketh.net

"Some of the very best teachers were once some of the very best students. Benedicte demonstrates that in her first book, The Key to A Richer Life. Drawing on the many lessons she learned as an avid student of personal development, from a varied collection of sageful teachers, she capably synthesize her experience into an outstanding guide to squeezing all of the life out of life. Read it with the expectation that its going to challenge your thinking, because it most definitely will!"

~

~ Lisa Jimenez - Author of International Best Seller, "Conquer Fear!"

"The first step in manifesting your dreams is to 'Master Your Mind'! In Benedicte's book, "THE KEY to a RICHER LIFE," she teaches you how. Begin your journey of creating your best life and read this book."

~

THE KEY to a RICHER LIFE - **Rating: 5.0 stars**

~ Lisa Ryan for **Readers Favorite**

"In her book "THE KEY to a RICHER LIFE" Benedicte Frölich takes the reader on a journey of personal growth through making better choices, accepting personal responsibility for the things that happen, and having the courage to pursue dreams, no matter what others have to say. Frölich discusses the importance of having the courage to go against the community, to ignore backstabbing, and to break away from damaging relationships. Unfortunately, there are many times when we make up excuses as to why we can't complete a task, or why something isn't our fault. If we want to experience a richer life, we need to get over ourselves, take responsibility for EVERYTHING, and keep moving forward.

I enjoyed reading the book as several of the chapters hit home in my experiences as an entrepreneur. She quotes many of my favorite authors including Napoleon Hill, David Schwartz, Wallace Wattles, Zig Ziglar and Mary Manin Morrissey, effortlessly weaving their words of wisdom into the chapter lessons. She doesn't sugar-coat her message - she is convinced that we have the ability to create whatever we want out of life, and she leads the reader to believe that it is so."

~

~ B. Allen - 5 stars

"Having studied many of the same "Great Teachers" of thought and philosophy over the years, I believe the author Benedicte Frölich has produced a truly inspiring and unique piece. She takes the reader on a personal journey of thought and reflection that must be experienced to be understood. Bravo Benedicte, this work is destined to become one of the great works in the field."

~

~ Peter Steidl - 5 stars - Great mix of actionable advice and real life illustrations

"I get most satisfaction from a book when the author makes the journey through the subject matter a personal one. This brings the material alive, engages and tests concepts and ideas against the realities of life.
Frölich says she has spent many years reading, listening to, and learning from the best in the field of personal development. No doubt she has: her book is rich with quotes and even personal messages she received from some recognized thoughtleaders.
But I am pleased to say that her book is much more than just a summary of what others said. It is full of examples and illustrations, often taken from her own life. By offering deep insights into her own journey she provides a rich context for the extensive material presented.
If you want to read about personal development then this is the book for you! It will not just engage, but captivate you and leave you a different person."

~

~ *Scot Conway* - 5 stars - Five Stars for Chapter 13 alone!

"I'm a man, so when I got to Chapter 13 about sex and saw it was written for women, I thought about glossing over it and jumping to chapter 14. It ended up capturing my attention and prompted discussion with my wife. This is a subject that she says does plague many women, and that she also thinks the solution is very much what the book is talking about. If Chapter 13 can lead many women to enjoy themselves so much more, then so will the men - and that, alone, is worth the five stars!

I was particularly drawn in by the Surgeon's Boat story in Chapter 7. So long at the dreaming was just fantasy, everyone could dream with him. Once he stepped up and actually made his dream a reality, suddenly people turned on him. Isn't that so often the case? That, and the "lucky" comments. A friend of mine kicked herself into high gear and did three years of school in one year, and as she graduated early so many of her friends remarked on how "lucky" she was to be finished early.

It's a good book over all. It's filled with some pretty solid, practical advice. Most people who read a lot of books on various facets of "success" will recognize much of what it is said - always good things to be reminded of (since none of us actually does 100% of what we "know"). One good idea from any book makes it worthwhile, and being reminded of a great many good ideas is even better. I might have given it four stars, but the conversation starter found in Chapter 13 (and few of us can have conversations like that without a conversation starter) is worth the five stars. May that chapter make a difference for couples all over the globe...."

~

(For more reviews go to: http://www.amazon.com/dp/B009K7S2L8)

DEDICATION

This book is dedicated to my fantastic husband and my two mentors M.H. and Chloe with the greatest and deepest love, gratitude and respect.

KNOWLEDGE is the key to something more, something bigger!

Knowledge creates a new and better understanding.

Knowledge opens new doors.

When I talk about the KEY to a richer life, it is the knowledge about yourself that I'm referring to, your strengths and unique abilities and, not least, knowledge and understanding of your powers of thought!

The understanding that *"You are and get what you think"* is *the* key that opens the door to the most amazing life;

> - a life overflowing on all levels!

The key to how you can create and live life TOTALLY, in all its beautiful and amazing nuances!

~

THERE IS A RESPONSIBILITY TO BE TAKEN

- AND A LIFE TO BE LIVED!

Benedicte Frölich

CONTENTS

- FOREWORD by BOB PROCTOR   11

- INTRODUCTION   13

1. THE FIRST STEP TOWARDS A BETTER LIFE   23

2. WHY ACCEPT A LIFE IN THE SHADOWS?   31

3. WHY ARE YOU ALLOWING YOURSELF TO BE PRESSURIZED?   44

4. BELIEVE IN YOURSELF!   49

5. YOU ARE AND RECIEVE WHAT YOU'RE THINKING ABOUT!   56

6. TAKE RESPONSIBILITY!   65

7. COURAGE   83

8. HOPELESSNESS/HOPE   91

9. LIVING IN THE EXTREMES   99

10. THE LUDICROUS WITHIN THE POSITIVE
    AND THE NEGATIVE   111

11. "THE RED BELL PEPPERS"   118

12. WHAT'S ACTUALLY THE WORST THAT CAN HAPPEN?   131

13. THE GENDER POWER STRUGGLE –
    AND WHERE DOES SEX FIT INTO THE EQUATION?   141
14. WHAT IS IT LIKE TO "ENJOY"?   151

15. *WHOSE* LIFE ARE YOU LIVING? –
    FOR *WHOSE* SAKE DO YOU DO THE THINGS YOU DO?   160

16. I HAVE ALL THAT I WANT IN MY LIFE!   173

17. WHAT HAS YOUR UPBRINGING MEANT FOR YOU?   185

  - FOR PERSONAL NOTES AND COMMENTS   191

  - THANK YOU   193

  - ABOUT THE AUTHOR   194

~

FOREWORD BY BOB PROCTOR

The Key to a Richer Life by Benedicte Frölich

There is a certain inherent magic in the image of a key. It's a thing so small, yet possessed of such great power and promise. A golden, glittering key conjures images of wonders and possibilities awaiting our discovery. It is, perhaps, the ultimate symbol of freedom.

In this marvelous volume, Benedicte Frölich promises you not just any old key, but THE key. The one that will unlock the gates to what you, I, and every living person is divinely designed to desire: A richer life.

Yet she does not propose to give you the key to these riches. After all, she doesn't have to. She knows what you will come to know as you travel along the path she sets out for you in these pages. *You already have this key*. It exists-and always has existed-inside of you.

What Benedicte does give you here is the treasure map that will lead you to that magical tool within yourself.

Benedicte has spent years studying the great seekers and thinkers, both of our own time and times past. She has absorbed their lessons wonderfully, and applied them with tremendous success in her own life. Her ability to communicate their wisdom with both understanding and authority makes her a perfect guide for this journey. With each step you take along the way, and each piece of wisdom you absorb, you will dissolve the mental layers that prevent you from seeing and embracing your own extraordinary creative power.

Throughout this book, you will repeatedly be confronted with the concept of choice-both in realizing that you have chosen the life you are living now, and in anticipation of the fact that, just as consciously and deliberately as you chose to pick up this book and read these words, you can choose to create the life you really want. If you don't fully believe that now, by the end of this marvelous book, you WILL.

You will also know *how* to do so.

What will your life of riches look like? You already have the answer. You've seen it in your dreams; you've explored it in your heart. It is there, alive, fully formed, as beautiful as you've imagined, and just waiting to welcome you into it.

You were born rich ... rich in potential and resources. You have deep reservoirs of talent and ability lying within. Find your key. Enter that life of your dreams and claim your riches. Let the wonderful Benedicte Frölich show you how.

Bob Proctor

Best-selling Author of *You Were Born Rich*

INTRODUCTION

What does it mean to be living a *RICHER* life, on all levels and in all its nuances?

What is it that holds us back with this life, these relationships and situations that we find ourselves in, despite all our dreaming of something entirely different, something better?

Why do we expose ourselves and thereby those we love and care for, to a life only half lived, when we actually *can* get it all, we *can* live life to the fullest?

Imagine, instantly experiencing the consequences of all your thoughts and actions!

Imagine, for example, immediately experiencing the consequences of one's lifestyle and eating habits!

Imagine if lung cancer appeared after only the first cigarette, obesity and cardio-vascular diseases after only the first burger, if financial ruin or bankruptcy came about after only the first little mistake or wrong decision, if the relationships or marriages broke down after the first instance of not respecting differences, or of attempts at controlling or putting the other person down!

But it doesn't!

Maybe that is the very reason why *so* many "let it slide". Often it isn't until the damage *is* already done, until the disease *has* become so alarming, or "the hole" we are in is *so* deep, or until the worst case scenario is *too* close, that we take a second look at our lives, our modes of thinking and acting.

We all have our concepts/paradigms, and our fixed modes of thinking and acting and it is all too often that we let them rule our lives, or that we allow our "here and now" situation and our outside influences to direct and control our moods and our lives! Why is it that so many people choose this, when in reality we can decide ourselves whether it will be the outside influences or ourselves who will run our lives?

So few have learnt to believe in themselves, or to really believe in and uncompromisingly strive for achieving their own dreams and aspirations in order to create the most amazing and richer life, on all levels.

All the way back to the early philosophers, thinkers and scientists, there have been writings about these fundamental "principles of life"- *We become what we think! You are and you will receive what you are thinking about! Your thoughts affect your mind, your mind your emotions, your emotions your actions and your actions your results!*

In recent times, one of the pioneers was Earl Nightingale. He has also been called "The Dean of Personal Development" and in 1956 he recorded, what was to be one of the first of its kind and definitely *the* most selling spoken word record outside the entertainment industry, "*The Strangest Secret*".

In a very short time, it sold more than one million copies!

Nightingale's recording, as well as books like "*As a Man Thinketh*" by James Allen and "*Think and Grow Rich*" by Napoleon Hill contributed to a break-through for the modern approach to this fundamental and seminal knowledge of "nature's laws and forces" and man's capacity for determining and guiding his own life and development.

The knowledge and understanding of how to take control over one's thoughts and thereby being able to create a better life for oneself, as well as for others, has now become available for the benefit of anyone interested.

Names like James Allen, Napoleon Hill, Earl Nightingale, Wallace D. Wattles, Jim Rohn, Bob Proctor, Zig Ziglar, Brian Tracy and Denis Waitley are undoubtedly the most world-renowned motivational experts. They, as well as the ever growing group of "younger" persons like Vic Johnson, Lisa Jimenez, Gerry Robert (all of whom are among my personal favourites), and *many, many* more, have contributed significantly to and further developed the fundamental principles by delving deep into their personal experiences and knowledge and thereby creating even more awareness about this subject.

I have long been missing a book like this translated into Danish and several times I have been encouraged to write one myself! So it has happened! It proves what I've learnt: that if you can't find what you are looking for, you'll just have to create it yourself!

For more than 20 years I have read, listened to, studied with and learned from the best within this field of personal development and *this* book is founded on their knowledge, as well as on my own personal work and experiences. My personal mentors have studiously "kept me on track" and even more than that, have held me accountable for my work and my continued development. They constitute without a doubt the biggest and most important reason for my being where I am today, armed with the knowledge and experience I have acquired!

Having someone who has walked the path all the way, who knows what it takes, who can help by asking the right questions and furthermore hold you responsible for the work you have embarked upon, is crucial for the success of it. Unless you yourself (as only extremely few have demonstrated) have the strength and/or the reasons to fight the fights that *must* be fought and take the steps that *have* to be taken!

I have learnt, copied and borrowed from the best and I have written this book by using my own words and experiences. I am sure the book will be a great source of inspiration, and motivation for many people to begin taking their lives seriously. I am also convinced it will be a great help to those who wish to create and thereby *LIVE* the *RICHEST* and most amazing life imaginable!

When we are discussing the *richer* life, it is also important that we come to terms with what lifestyle is all about and what it represents for each of us. One of the things Jim Rohn said is that *Lifestyle is more about how we choose to live and how we choose to design our lives!* Many use their low income or a poor financial situation as a reason or an excuse for their bad or negative attitude. They claim that once their finances get better *then* they'll show us what happiness and cheerfulness is!

But happiness and being content is something that we choose!

This is one of the basic facts, which more often than not arouse dissent and, yes, sometimes almost indignation because how can you be happy when one's economy is deplorable, or one's relationship(s) is (are) not working out, etc.?

The unique feeling of contentment, which many mistakenly believe will only appear when we achieve our goals, must come before the success because it is itself a main reason for the success.

Take note here of the fundamental "principles of life": *We become what we think! You are and receive what you are thinking about! and so on.*

You can begin by asking yourself whether your situation improves, or whether your problems are being solved by you being angry, sad, irritated or sorry.

They aren't, are they?

So instead of being angry, sad or frustrated, why not choose to be happy and positive and make the best of the situation as it is?

In other words, we can *choose* to experience happiness and contentment, despite our current situations or circumstances.

If we don't learn how to be content in our present situation, we will never be happy no matter how much happiness and luck we may encounter! So when we are talking about lifestyle, it is a question of *living* more, living more fully, with more awareness and consciousness, living with more contentment, and living with a more overall appreciation, respect and gratitude. Living life to the fullest! Living *NOW!*

The fuller the life we live, the more we will be inspired to do and the more we achieve the more we shall receive! So lifestyle is how you design and create a unique life! As I have said, it is a skill to be learnt, not a condition to be chased after!

It is the ability to find new ways of bringing contentment, excitement, pleasure and substance into our own everyday life, as well as into that of those we love, *while* we are working to achieve our goals, and not merely when we *have* achieved them!

If we are not content, or fail to thrive in our present situation, the only way we can start changing it is by changing the way we think and feel.

We do not have to be (financially) rich to live a richer life!

All the happiness and satisfaction that we wish for can be ours right now – merely by changing how we think and feel about the concept of lifestyle.

Lifestyle is also about learning to *be*, wherever you *are*! It is about developing a unique focus on the *now* and learning how to extract all the richness and substance from the experiences and feelings that the *now* affords.

Lifestyle is not something we do, or something we have; it is something we experience and until we learn to live and to be *present* in the now, we will not be able to master the art of living a *RICHER* and *FULLER* life.

Our lifestyle presents a clear picture of who we are and how we are thinking!

Keep in mind that we are attracting more of what we are thinking about into our own lives – be it positive or negative! It is very important that we are conscious about our thoughts and that we learn to master them!

Remember that if you just continue doing what you have always done, you'll continue receiving what you have always received!

It's as simple as that!

Small and "innocent" as they may seem, acts that by themselves seem to be harmless and that do not create any "here and now" problems can, if repeated often or on a daily basis, and if they are not conducive to your health, your financial situation, your relationships, or your life in general, in the long run do so much damage that it will require an even larger effort to correct the situation!

Even an almost invisible or minimal change of course in the wrong direction will, if not corrected, gradually steer your "ship" off course towards certain calamity.

On the other hand, any progressive and positive act in the right direction, however small it may seem, will, *if repeated daily*, just as surely steer your life towards your goals!

If you really *want* change, development, success and wealth, it takes a continued and *daily* effort!

So, whether it is the course that needs to be set and continuously corrected with a focus on the goal, or it is your "garden" that needs tending to keep the weeds away, your thoughts *must* be "tended", so that the "mental weeds" will not be allowed to take over and run your life.

We are all unique and we all possess unique and fantastic features. We all have our own values and qualities, our own goals and dreams!

We can *all* change our lives for the better – but it takes effort!

This book has been written to be an inspiration and a motivation to help see and have the belief that it is possible to take control over your own life. That change, development and growth *is* possible, no matter *where* we might find ourselves in our lives right now!

All the chapters in this book have been written as small self-contained units, or training modules, if you like, predominantly worked out from a main theme. As much of the material builds on the same fundamental principles, there will be things and thoughts that will reappear in the individual chapters.

This will add more angles and perhaps facilitate a better understanding of the principles! You can read the book as you see fit.

Take a chapter at a time from start to finish and then work with the thoughts and questions that arise along the way. Or you can use the book as an encyclopaedia, where you pick a chapter that deals with some of the things you need in relation to where you are in your life right now.

No matter how you approach this book, I would recommend that you take a break after each chapter and in the light of what you have just read, reflect on your own relationships and your own life.

Try posing critical and personal questions about your own choices and your own modes of thinking and acting and thereby get a better understanding of your choices and also about how you can turn your present, seemingly hopeless, situation into an important learning process that can take you further on in your personal development and in the creation of the most amazing life you can imagine!

It is my experience that the same text or training will be read, re-read, understood or experienced in relation to where you, at that given moment, are in your personal development!

I will, therefore, encourage you to come back to the book again and again and each time you read it, you will understand something new and something more!

A good many will read this book and nod knowingly at what I am writing:

Yeah, yeah! I know THAT! I've heard THAT before! I've tried THAT before!

At this point I will remind you of the ever so true words: *To know, but not to do is not to know!*

There is after all a reason for your being where you are and for having what you have in your life!

It is one thing to understand it intellectually but it is an entirely different matter to incorporate it into our hearts and our subconscious, and to start *LIVING* it!

That's why this book, as well as all the inspiration and wisdom you may receive from me and everybody else sharing their experiences in this field, is meant to motivate and inspire you in your daily thought processes. It has been written in the hope that *you* will also create and enjoy a most amazing and *RICHER* life and that you will live it *to the full*, on all levels and in all its nuances!

You need to know and believe that all the possibilities are already there, lying at your feet!

If your desire is strong enough and if you have reasons enough in your life to want change, then the first thing that is required is a *DECISION!*

On top of that you'll have to add:

COURAGE – to acknowledge where you are in your life and why!

STRENGTH – to act, daring to opt out and go against the flow – and last but not least to *PERSEVERE* – to keep doing it again and again, right up "until ..."!

This is the formula for success within any area of your life!

But much more about this in the following chapters.

Here you are holding *THE KEY* to a richer life!

Now it is entirely up to you – how you use it and what you'll do with your life!

Remember... *YOUR LIFE IS YOUR RESPONSIBILITY!*

~

Personal notes and comments:

CHAPTER 1

THE FIRST STEP TOWARDS A BETTER LIFE

If you really *want* to change, then surely the first step *is* to just take a decision, isn't it?

But when should you get started?

When should you react and more specifically, when should you act?

Sadly, most of the time we have to get all the way out there, or down there, where we feel we've reached the bottom, before we get down to it and take the decision(s) needed, for example, if you are suddenly diagnosed with a serious or even life threatening illness, or if you feel you can't fall any further and *now* it can't get any worse. That is, when you are fed up with feeling fed up, when you think *either I give up, curl up and die or I fight this!*

But doesn't it begin long before this? Shouldn't we already react when the first signs of dissatisfaction surface when you sense that you are not thriving or that you are unsatisfied with your situation – at work for example, or with your family, your relationships, your home, your financial situation, or your life in general. Then you may have thoughts and emotions such as these: *Is this the right thing, after all? Is this really where I want to be? There must be more in this for me!*

It is actually good not to just settle for something. Know that you can sense this uneasiness or dissatisfaction because this may be the seed that makes you one day decide to do something about it, and motivate you to seek and find the courage, the strength and the means to do something about your discontentment!

Since our children were small my husband and I have taught them not only that they are fantastic and unique, that they are loved unconditionally and that they should have belief in themselves, but also that they should never settle for less.

They should not settle for, or accept, second best. We want them to learn to strive for more and better, to know that they deserve only the best and to believe that they *can* have what they want, because this is how you create the foundation for progress in life!

It is always important to focus on creating a good and solid foundation! It is not enough just to be well grounded physically – for a heavy, static and intractable person can neither carry out nor relish changes! Many are so deeply attached to what they've got that they daren't let go!

If the winds of change are blowing, you can become extremely vulnerable, because even the slightest change or adjustment (for example at work) will seem almost life threatening!

I remember a story I once heard about a boat named *Wave Dancer*. She was tightly moored in a harbour since very rough weather was brewing. A tornado warning had been issued in that very area. The captain and the crew thought they would be best protected on board the boat, so it was secured to the best of their abilities and tightly moored to the quay. All the guests on board were calm because now they believed that they were safe and sound. All they had to do now was to just wait for the storm to blow over.

But "poor" *Wave Dancer*, who was now tightly lashed to the quay, could not ride the waves the way a boat is designed to, and she was smashed to pieces and everybody on board drowned.

So rather than the outside influences, what you should ensure is that your personal foundation is strong and solid.

If you have *belief* in yourself and your abilities, *belief* in and *knowledge* of *who* you are and *what* you can do and of course, – very importantly, *what* you want, then it will be impossible to knock you off course. Temporary setbacks might shake you up a bit, but they will not be able to bring you down for good.

Instead of being scared out of your wits, you will be able to face changes and new challenges with the curiosity of a small child, who discovers for the first time, something new and exciting.

The child would want to do it all: observe, touch, taste and experiment!

If *you* succeed in steering your life and your relationships with others in this way, if you learn to take things in your stride, it will make way for new experiences, new acquaintances and new possibilities that you had never even imagined!

From a very young age and throughout their childhood, children often hear: *NO! You can't do that! Don't do that! You'll get hurt! You'll fall down! Be careful! Let go of that! It'll break! Mummy and Daddy are getting upset now! Behave! Sit quietly! Oh! Look how clumsy you are! Look what you've done now! You'll never learn this! You can't do THAT! You are way too small, fat, ugly, stupid, etc.*

Many of these children accept this as the truth about who they are and what they are able to do and it stays with them all the way into adult life, where they will pass it in turn on to their own children. So not only does the child learn that new things are dangerous, difficult, forbidden and "hands off", they also learn that they cannot, may not, and are no good!

How is a person supposed to venture out and meet the world, face the new challenges and exciting things which life of course entails and which will surface time and again, if one has no belief in oneself and one's own abilities or, if the *courage* to explore and experiment isn't there?

James Allen says: *Belief is the basis for all action and this being so, the belief that dominates the heart or mind is shown in life!*

You will only very rarely try something that you already don't believe to be possible. You will never give one hundred per cent of your capacity to something you don't believe in! It is not necessarily one specific thing or possibility that you don't believe in, even though there may already be overwhelming proof that it can be done; for example, the fact that others before you have previously had success with that particular work or project.

But if you don't have belief in yourself, you will, as I've previously said, never give 100% and everything; the project, your new job, your dream of becoming independent, etc., will fail and fall flat and you will convince yourself that this is not something for you, that *you* can't do it, or don't deserve it!

David J Schwartz, author of *"The Magic of Thinking Big"* says: *The size of your success is determined by the size of your belief!*

This is as true as it can be and this constitutes one of the first and most important elements in the understanding and creation of a better and richer life!

The day you really understand this message, the day it really enters your heart and you understand the depth and the meaning of it, you will know what you need to work on, to achieve a better life; *your belief in yourself!*

Lisa Jimenez writes in the book *"Conquer Fear"*: *If you change your belief you will change your behaviour! If you change your behaviour you will change your results! If you change your results you will change your life!*

If you have heard a lot of negative and condescending statements for example: *You can't do that! You're no good! You can never do anything right! You are too dumb, too small, too big, too fat, too clumsy, etc.*, you may well have fixed certain limitations about yourself and what you really, actually can do! It can then be difficult to believe that there *is* something bigger and better for you than the life you are currently living.

But by being the unique person you are, there *are always* new, exciting possibilities and experiences in store! You don't even have to know *how*; you just need to know *what* you want! Secondly, you must know and find your *why*!

According to an old adage: *When you truly believe that you can do it – then you can do it and the "how to" will follow!*

Precisely this very question *How?* is often a big, if not *the* biggest, stumbling block for most people. Far too many people attempt to figure out *everything* in advance, before they have the courage to embark upon something new! But how can you know *how*, when you have never even tried it before? It's like attempting to cross the finishing line, *before* you have even started the race!

Another of Earl Nightingale's sayings: *Don't concern yourself too much with how you are going to achieve your goal, leave that completely to a power greater than yourself! All you have to do is know where you're going! The answers will come to you of their own accord and at the right time!*

The sooner you understand and accept what amongst others Earl Nightingale, David J Schwartz and Lisa Jimenez have said, the sooner you can start reaching out for and create the very life that you want!

If there are any modes of thinking or acting that have accompanied you "automatically", maybe even passed down from generation to generation, then it is up to you to break them, and to create your own truths, truths that will fit *your* own life, your reality!

They could be very small and "*innocent*" things we are doing without really thinking about *why*!

As this little story illustrates:

A man is asked to fetch the Sunday Joint that he and his wife had ordered at the butcher's, but when he returns home, his wife discovers that the butcher has forgotten to slice off the ends of the joint, as they always ask him to do.

At first the wife scolds her husband for not paying attention to this, but the husband, keeping his cool, a bit puzzled, asks his wife: *Precisely why do the ends have to be cut off?*

Still a bit annoyed over her husbands' negligence at the butcher's, the wife says: *Why, we are used to having it done!*

At this the husband replies: *Yes, I know that, but precisely why?*

The wife ponders the question and answers: *We've just always done it! I learnt that from my mother.*

How about calling your mother and asking her why she did it? the husband suggests.

The wife, who by now has calmed down, says yes, she can do that, because she has actually also begun wondering about it.

The mother answers: *Why, we have always done that! I learnt that from my mother.*

Now, fortunately for this story, the grandmother was still alive, so the young woman calls up her grandmother and asks her the same question: *Precisely why is it that we cut the ends off the Sunday Joint, before we put it into the oven?* Her grandmother ponders for a while and then she says: *Well, I guess it's because our oven was so small, that there never was space for a whole Sunday Joint.*

Something which *back then* had a perfectly natural reason and justification had become a habit, something which today would not even be thought about or questioned.

Try looking with new and curious eyes at your life and at your habits, or at what you think or say.

IS there anything at all that fits in, or is the right thing for you and is functioning well in your life right now?

Maybe it is about time to pause and do a bit of clearing out of the *We are used to...! That's just how it is!*

If there are things in your life, your relationships, your situation, which you are not content with, or aren't thriving with, maybe it is because you need to shake yourself up a bit and have the guts to break the old habits that tie you down!

This particularly goes for your belief and opinions about yourself. At the very least you must find out what it is that you want with your life so that you can take the decision to go after it and create it!

Remember – *whatever you don't change, your children inherit!*

What kind of life is it that you wish for yourself and for them?

THAT IS WORTH THINKING ABOUT!

~

Personal notes and comments:

CHAPTER 2

WHY SETTLE FOR A LIFE IN THE SHADOWS?

Why settle for a life in the shadows, when the most fantastic life – sun-enriched and filled to the brim on all levels – is lying right there at your feet?

When the fact is that you are standing in front of the largest "feast", that ever was!

Life is like The Horn of Plenty always remaining full, in fact you will come to discover that the more you take from it, the more it will produce!

You are facing a life, where you can choose contentment and happiness *every* day!

WHO says that life has to be tough?

Our limited thought processes are restricting *our* lives, nothing else and nobody else!

If you always try to find the causes, or put the blame for your problems and shortcomings on others, and on external circumstances, you are thoroughly mistaken. It may look as if it is the others who are limiting you but most likely you can surely make a list of things and causes as to why you are, where you are now – in a sad, hard, unhappy life, always in the shadows.

But when it comes down to it, it is your choice. *You* choose to accept the explanations and excuses as the final truth!

You deprive yourself of the possibility of choosing to live a fulfilling life, because you have accepted the life you now have as the only alternative.

This doesn't mean that you are doing it out of happiness or contentment – who would consciously do or choose that?

What many people forget is that this universe is built and governed by certain fixed and essential laws, for example the *Law of Gravity* – one of those laws that, we know beyond a doubt, affect all and sundry. It makes no difference who or what you are, whether you are a good and warm hearted human being, who is always positive, always giving and helping others, or whether you are living the most miserable life, always negative, a cold and cynical person. You know that if you fell off a tall tower, you would hit the ground and be killed.

Two people who have inspired me immensely – and still do – are Brian Tracy and Bob Proctor, who, like many others, talk about *The Laws of the Universe*, and how they affect our everyday lives.

We are living with these laws of nature every day, yet a lot of people are not even faintly aware of them, despite the fact that they influence us just the same way as they do everybody else.

The fact is that you can't change what you don't know! But also the more you learn, the more you realise there are things that you didn't know! That is simply the way it is! This is the reason

I have decided that I, for the rest of my life, will explore, learn and study so that I can continuously grow and develop!

I can see how amazing my life has become, now that I have taken responsibility for it and have acquired a larger and better understanding of, among other things, some of the laws of the universe! However, at the same time, I have come to realize that I've only just begun "scratching the surface."

Another of the basic laws in this universe affecting our lives and our well-being is *The Law of Control*. Most psychologists have concluded that our mental health is directly proportional to the degree of control we feel we have over ourselves and our life.

It is to be understood that to the extent to which we feel good about ourselves, we feel we are having control over our own life; or on the contrary, we feel bad about ourselves, or feel out of harmony with ourselves to exactly the same degree that we feel controlled by external circumstances, other people, things or causes.

Another law is the *Law of Accident* or *Coincidence*, a law that describes how and why we don't feel that we are in control of what is happening to us, or what is going on around us. We feel like a ball in a game of pool where we are knocked randomly here and there, out of control and into the pockets.

These feelings of being subject to coincidence and the lack of control on our own lives are, according to many experts, one of the main reasons why we experience so much negativity, disharmony, grief, annoyance, dissatisfaction, unhappiness and scepticism in our lives, as well as in the world of today. Naturally, people who are merely living by, or letting themselves and their lives be ruled by outside influences or coincidences, will not feel that they are in control of either their life or of their mental well being.

If you haven't set yourself any goals to strive after in your life, you will easily be subject to these laws, as it is said: *If you fail to plan, you plan to fail*!

Another important law of nature is the *Law of Cause and Effect*. This is one of the fundamental laws of nature that affects *everything* that is happening in our lives.

There is a defining cause for everything that is happening and if we don't like these actions, results, or consequences we are facing in our lives, it is up to *us* to identify these causes and change them! Even though we can't immediately see or understand what the cause of these different events in our lives may be, there always *is* a cause for whatever happens!

It is also important for us to know and remember that there is *always* a lesson to be learnt, in whatever we are exposed to!

Control begins first and foremost with our thoughts, with *what* we are thinking, because that affects and leads to our emotions and whatever we feel will affect and lead to our actions! So *all* control will begin with our taking control over our own thoughts!

You will, therefore, have to make up your mind about what *you* want with your life! Set your goals and pursue them!

The biggest goal in life that one can aspire to must be to achieve total peace of mind!

To be able to live peacefully and in harmony with oneself and one's surroundings!

To have physical and mental reserves! To be free from fear, anger and guilt – probably the three strongest and most destructive thoughts and emotions of all!

Then you can pursue physical well-being – good health and a high energy level and create loving and long lasting relationships with your partner, family, friends, etc.

My wish is that you will strive for and achieve all the best things here in life! That you will also have success and abundance on all levels, because I know that then *you* will be able to go on to help and enthuse even more people, once you personally have reached your own goals in life!

You have to help yourself before you can help others! Once you personally have experienced how amazing life is in all its nuances and what possibilities lie in wait at your and at everybody else's feet, then you will be better at helping, guiding and inspiring others to do what you personally have done.

Create your own amazing life filled with peace, contentment and abundance, and then you can go out and help and inspire even more on *their* journey!

One of the greatest delights is to be able to contribute to making a difference for others! Bear in mind that this can be done in many different ways!

True wealth is not just about money and material things!

True wealth is about a *RICHER* life – one that *is* accessible to all!

There is enough of everything and there is enough for all!

Life *is* a great feast, a Horn of Plenty of possibilities and abundance on all levels for everyone to enjoy!

The possibilities are infinite because ideas are infinite and every idea can be transformed into wealth, which in turn can be invested in new projects and can thus be of help to others!

Who is to say that there is not enough to go around, that we shouldn't take too much?

Who is tying us down in these somewhat boring, or even dismal and miserable lives?

What is it that makes us accept that life *has to* be tough and that there is not enough to go around?

Try to imagine that the entire population of the Earth simultaneously took a deep breath and *held it*! Wouldn't there still be air left? We *can't* take too much because by using our ideas and thoughts, we *can* create everything that is needed and much more!

When we are living in a society and a world where everything *should* be possible why is it that so few are actually utilising the enormous possibilities? The vast majority of people are living a life of quiet desperation. They are dissatisfied with their jobs, their relationships, and their health; they are overweight; they smoke or drink too much; and take pain killers and anti-depressants like candy. They generally live a dismal, depressing and restrictive life!

There are only about 5% of people who manage to follow their dreams, manage to set themselves goals, learn from their mistakes and constructively use challenges and setbacks to grow and become stronger! Only a very few realise their full potential and what it takes to go "all the way"!

Only a very few understand that it is about taking responsibility for your own life, your own actions! Taking control over your thoughts is taking control over your actions so that it is *you* who is steering you towards the life you want!

Why?

It might be because we are not born with a manual describing *man's* full potential and providing guidelines for an ideal and *richer* life!

Most of us have, from infancy and throughout our formative years, come to believe that life *is* tough, that there is not enough for everybody, that money doesn't grow on trees, etc. because that is precisely what our parents, their parents and their parents before them, have taught and passed down.

Today you will find regions where people have been on social welfare for 4 or 5 generations because that is "simply" the way it is!

The children are taught not to "fight" for anything, but believe that they can just sit back and give up in advance, doomed to a life without an education, without jobs and without any hope for the future! They grow up believing that there is not enough for everybody; some get more than enough, or everything, whilst the vast majority has very little, or nothing at all!

It requires extraordinary strength, but occasionally we do hear about people who manage to break free of their bonds, rise up, seek new challenges and go after their own dreams, people who refuse to accept their predicament and who believe that there is more to life, despite what their parents, friends and colleagues constantly tell them.

It may be that your parents don't know how to get ahead themselves, because their parents have said the same things to them: *Who do you think you are? How can you possibly think, that you can just waltz in and do it? You can't make a living from that! Be realistic! You've got to eat! There'll be bills to pay! Only rich people can do that! You'll never be successful! Imagine everybody just doing what they please, then society would fall apart!*

We cannot and should not blame them or others for holding us back, because their reaction is merely conditioned by what they personally have heard and what they personally have come to believe in.

But if you stop and look around, you will easily find examples of rich and successful people who are by far lacking in your abilities, your intelligence, your strength, or your good looks, but who, despite this, have reached their goals and achieved great success and wealth!

Anybody *can* do it! All it takes is for you to believe in it and to believe in yourself!

It all begins with you taking a decision, the decision to go all the way, no matter what! No matter what other people may think or say, no matter what, "*we are used to doing in our family!*" No matter what the odds look like, no matter what *your situation or life might look like right now! None* of this has any relevance for what *you* can achieve, but you have to want it, have belief in it and you have to change your way of thinking, so that you can thereby change you actions and achieve a new result! Because if you keep doing the same things you have always done, you will continue receiving what you have always received!

Throughout history we have been given plenty of examples showing us what we really are capable of doing, *if* there are no limitations! The only limitations are the ones we have in our heads and those are the ones that tie us down! They are our own beliefs and thoughts about what we can't achieve and why we can't achieve it!

I am sure we are all familiar with the story of the bumble bee. Many people realise that theoretically it shouldn't be able to fly (the heavy body versus the small wingspan). But still it flies! Jokingly we say the reason why it flies is that it doesn't know it can't!

If we act without limitations, there are no limits as to what we can achieve or receive in this life!

Another example is the story about the young student George

Dantzig, as told by Cynthia Kersay in her book "*Unstoppable*":

As a young college student George was studying very hard as always until late into the night, so late that one day he overslept and was twenty minutes late for class. He assumed that the two mathematical problems on the blackboard were the next assignment, so he quickly copied them down.

It took him several days to work himself through the two problems, but finally he managed to solve them and he delivered the papers to his professor the following day.

A few days later (early one Sunday morning), George was woken up by a very excited professor. Because George had been late for class, he hadn't heard the professor explain that the two equations on the black board were two mathematical problems that not even Einstein had been able to crack!

But George Dantzig, who was working without any kind of limitations to his thinking, managed to solve not one, but both the problems, which mathematicians had been struggling with for centuries! In short, George solved them because he didn't know he couldn't!

There *is* ample evidence that others have been able to do it!

So, what is holding *you* back?

Are we going to permit others' beliefs about what is possible and right to determine how we are to live our lives, to determine what we are to believe and what is enjoyable and right for us?

~

Snoopy (from *Peanuts*) was out skating on a big lake. Smiling blissfully as only Snoopy can, he was skating around performing figures of eight and other tricks. When Lucy came by and asked condescendingly what on earth he was doing,

Snoopy proudly answered that he was ice skating, while elegantly gliding past Lucy on one leg.

But ... You are not wearing any skates! Lucy exclaimed looking condescendingly and almost spitefully at Snoopy. In the last picture we find Snoopy sitting in the snow by the lakeside looking very sad: *Drat! Just when I thought I was having so much fun!*

~

Take a look at your own life. Who are the "dream stealers" in *your* life?

We *all* have fantastic and special talents, hidden abilities and resources to tackle and solve all that we set our minds to, things we *want* and things we want to pursue! Once we have taken a decision about *what* it is that we want and start striving towards it, then it will automatically become clear *how* we will achieve it (*see Chapter 1*). When first our hearts and minds are set on what it is we want, or have to do, it is amazing to see how *our* brains begin to find solutions!

As I've previously mentioned, *you* are the only one who can limit and thereby stop yourself from achieving what *you* want out of life! It is a decision to be taken and *you* are the only one who can take that decision; *you* are the only one who can do that for yourself!

Why should you accept a life in the shadows, when you *can* have everything you want in this life? It is up to you. *Whose* life do you want to live? Do you want to live a life based upon what other people say you can and can't do, a life limited by what you *think* is possible, a life where you accept other people's limitations, a life where you allow family traditions and "we're used to" to define your happiness?

Far too many find refuge in absurdities, when they are looking for explanations and justifications as to precisely why it is that they just can't do that which they earlier proclaimed they really wanted to do.

Many also react strongly to the even more provocative truth that *we receive and attract into our lives, that which we are thinking about!*

Who deliberately wants adversity and a constant uphill struggle?

It's often much easier for us to find explanations and reasons for *not* doing what we really want to do. So, despite the fact that we are holding on to this difficult and problematic life we are living, it is the one that we are familiar with! We all have our comfort zone. Don't you often hear someone or even yourself saying: *It's better to have the devil you know, than the devil you don't know!?*

By not trying, by choosing to say no, we avoid risking defeat. Once again it is the safe and secure way instead of the exciting and the challenging way which might have been the way to a new and better life!

To grow you must be willing to let your present and your future be totally unlike your past! Your history is not your destiny! (Alan Cohen).

Bear in mind that we cannot change that which we have already experienced, or been subjected to. The deeds of the past cannot be changed, but we can change our view on what has happened and decide not to let it influence or control our lives and future anymore!

We must learn to forgive and move on!

Remember you can do *anything* you set your mind to!

So, pursue your dreams, step out of the shadows and pull away from everything and everybody that holds you back, or keeps you down.

Instead you should listen to and seek the advice and support from those who *have* already experienced it, rather than from those who have never dared themselves, or never believed in their own possibilities and dreams and who therefore (consciously or unconsciously) hold you back! Their thoughts will be that if *they* were unable, or not allowed to, you certainly shouldn't be able or allowed to either!

Listen to those who *have achieved* success. Learn from their experiences and as I've previously said, seek your support and guidance from those who you know will stand by you, those who believe in you because they, by having done it themselves, know that it *is* possible to achieve and acquire whatever you are going after!

Now you know we *all* have equal possibilities and that anybody can achieve anything they attempt to achieve, *if they decide to*, that there *is* enough for all, and that you *are* standing before life's great feast! Then why not take the chance, decide for yourself to *believe* in it and also to believe that you, given the right help, support and guidance, can do it!

Decide to move forward and to create a better life for yourself, a life full of love and filled to the brim on all levels!

TAKE CONTROL OF YOUR LIFE!

STEP OUT OF THE SHADOWS AND INTO THE LIGHT!

~

Personal notes and comments:

CHAPTER 3

WHY ARE YOU ALLOWING YOURSELF TO BE PRESSURIZED?

Yes, why are *you* allowing yourself to be pressurized?

Why does *anybody* allow themselves to be pressurized? In reality, it may well be that we are pressurizing ourselves the most, with our habitual thoughts and actions, which we've carried with us since early childhood, like doing things we don't really want to do, but which we *think* are necessary.

When I think back on it, when was I most vulnerable and easiest to be put under pressure? It was when I didn't know or believe in myself, my knowledge, my abilities, my feelings, or my desires. It was when I didn't know what *I* wanted!

When you are unsure about your own position, unsure about what will happen if you opt out, or say no, you will be easy to pressurize, and easy to convince that it has to be different, or that you most probably want what the others suggest!

If you too were raised in life's "charm school", then it won't exactly be *your* needs, feelings and desires that have been focused upon and maybe you are now a grown-up who still hasn't learnt to listen to and respect your own limits and worst of all, you may not even know them! Maybe you carry inside you all this uneasiness, discomfort, irritation, anger, and insecurity, which you can't really pinpoint and maybe all too often you take it out on the wrong people – your children, your husband, your wife, your colleagues – but actually it is just your own incomprehension of what is going on, or why so!

You might not even know where it comes from and definitely not what to do about it! How do you feel about yourself, when you let yourself be pressed into something that you don't really want or like to do?

Often we turn this anger towards ourselves because we really can't grasp what happened, or because we *once again* did something we really didn't want to do, or couldn't find the heart to say no! After all who else is there to blame but ourselves?

You may well know somebody, who (always) manages to let their own frustration out on somebody else. It could be a husband, who at home is being hassled by his wife, who in turn lets it out on an employee at work. Or they may take the hassles at work with them home to their families and take them out on their wives, yelling at the children and kicking the dog!

In far too many of such incidents, these people don't even know why they are reacting the way they do! They just have all this anger and frustration inside them.

You can be so entangled within your own web that you can't get out again. But then again, wasn't it you who initially failed to stand up for yourself, when he/she/it did something to you and over-stepped your limits?

Maybe you stood there with a feeling like: *Hey! What the**** just happened?* Now you feel that it is getting more and more difficult to draw the line because you've gone along with it a couple of times, so why suddenly opt out now? *You just can't do that!*

It could be visiting relations that is a pain, always ending up with the same arguments *every* time! It could be the mother in law, who interferes too much, without your spouse putting his or her foot down and taking your side, as he/she ought to!

Every time we do something that goes against our wishes or desires, this frustration and anger grows because we might have a notion that we are not allowed to place the feeling where it really belongs! Far too often it is taken out on the wrong people and more often than not in inappropriate ways!

Does it improve your boss or your mother in laws' way of treating you, if you bash yourself over the head, or even worse your next of kin? No, it doesn't, does it?

Have you ever noticed that when you are clear and well-focused about your situation, your point of view, your thoughts and your feelings, then it is easier to stand your ground? Then you won't be rattled or toppled; nor will you allow yourself to be manipulated or pressurized into doing something, that you do not really want to do!

Knowledge provides this calmness, this strength! Here I am not just alluding to knowledge about things or subjects, but more importantly, to knowledge about yourself! I am talking about *Self-awareness!*

Self-awareness is the key phrase here because it is not until you look deep within and discover yourself, your own limits, desires, needs and behavioural patterns, that you will be strong enough to withstand any pressure from others as well as from yourself!

When you know what *you* stand for, what *you* like and what *you* want, you're no longer an "easy victim"! Many have grown up without having learnt to believe in themselves, without being told that what *they* want, think, believe in, do, or can, is good enough!

If they have also heard that the most important things are to behave well, to please others and to never decline (often misunderstood to mean doing what others want regardless of it being in opposition to, or over-stepping your limits), then they become easy to exploit, pressurize and manipulate!

If you are thinking more about what others might be thinking than what is the right thing for you, then you are not living after your own values and in the end you won't have a clue as to what you really want, or stand for!

The only thing you feel is this destructive anger and this irritation with yourself and with others, which steadily eats you up from within!

The more often you manage to take a stand for yourself *and* discover that you actually survived it, the more you will be in harmony with yourself and your surroundings!

So, the first step is becoming aware of what *you* want, then of when and why you are doing things you don't want to do, and then finally, taking yourself and your limits seriously and acting accordingly!

Draw the line and stand fast!

Be proud of yourself, who you are, what you want and what *you* stand for! Then, no one can pressurize you! But you must realise that it needs practice; so being in doubt and a little insecure is ok. It *is* relatively new for you, so allow yourself to be uncertain, frightened and maybe even afraid.

Just as long as you do it!

Remember that it is only by repeating things over and over again that you learn to master a new discipline!

IT'S YOUR LIFE! LIVING IT RICHLY AND TO THE FULL IS ONE OF THE MOST IMPORTANT DISCIPLINES TO MASTER!

Personal notes and comments:

CHAPTER 4

BELIEVE IN YOURSELF!

What happens if you have no belief in yourself? Neither belief nor trust!

Far too many go through life with low self-esteem or with little or no confidence in themselves, a condition which for most people began in early childhood and which many people carry with them for the rest of their lives like a *heavy anchor*, which holds them back and prevents any kind of development! If belief has been removed, or you have never learnt to believe nor trust in yourself, you could easily become a "victim" for others, who either consciously or unconsciously chooses to exploit this (*See Chapter 3*).

This will affect so many areas of your life: your ability to love (both yourself and others), your personal relationships, your relationships with colleagues, friends and family, your job, your career possibilities, your life, and your lifestyle – yes, practically *everything*!

We have to go back in life a very long way, all the way back to early childhood, more specifically from about 1½ years of age to 6 or 7 but often many more times during later life, where things done or said to us by our parents or other people in authority, teachers, friends, colleagues, bosses, etc., have had such a deep impact that the belief in ourselves as the most amazing and unique beings that we all are is incredibly low, if not non-existent!

From very early on we may well have learnt that we, our opinions, our wishes and our dreams, are of no importance and that everything is about pleasing, satisfying and fulfilling the others' needs and wishes!

We may always have felt that we needed to be "on top of the situation," be mind readers, and figure out what the next move would have to be, to prevent, for example, our parents from getting angry, driven by the fear and anxiety of them not loving us anymore, the fear that they or friends might turn their backs on us, or that we would be abandoned or face rejection! These thoughts and fears can become so deep rooted that even today they blur our thoughts and rationality!

When the fear of not being good enough, of not doing something well enough, as well as the fear of being abandoned takes over, it is no longer your own free will or *your* needs that take priority. You may begin to become accustomed to pushing your own needs and wishes further and further aside and then the doubt arrives whether whatever *you* feel and prefer can be justified!

What happens when you again and again give others the impression that you desire the same as they (in order to please and to avoid being rejected), when you are not being true to yourself or honest with them?

You will end up being unable to trust anybody because how can you believe what others are saying to be true, if you are not being honest yourself? How can you trust them, when you are never telling the truth yourself? You have possibly heard the expression: *All thieves think everyone steals!*

This problem has far greater implications for your relationships and interactions with others than you might actually think! Therefore, you really need to think it through!

Another issue is the feelings we have about ourselves. Far too many go through life without learning to believe and to have trust in themselves and their own values, unable to learn to love themselves because their thinking is: *WHAT is there to love?*

But the fact is; we are not able to love others more than we love ourselves!

When you are constantly trying to figure out how to please others, you will end up *assuming* and *then* you really are on thin ice!

Think back a while. Have you *ever* succeeded in guessing correctly? Most will probably nod in agreement that they are not in contact with their own emotions when they are trying to figure out whatever it may be that others might want or wish!

As long as you are trying to "figure it out" and live by your assumptions, you can't feel what *you* really want! When you are in doubt about what you want, because amongst other things you have never learnt to cater for your own needs and desires, or to prioritize and value yourself and you don't feel that you can or are allowed to say *NO*, you can easily end up feeling man-handled and that of course can lead to even more damage and cause even deeper scars!

If you have repeatedly felt this kind of manipulation because you simply didn't dare draw the line, when you should have listened to yourself and respected your own limits, then *how* can you expect others to respect them?

If you are not "up front" in your approach then others can and may well misunderstand your agreement and your actions!

Then again, you have created a situation for yourself which gives others the impression of a person who allows others to walk all over them and exploit them!

This of course further undermines you self-esteem!

So the next time you find yourself in a situation where you feel powerless with respect to your needs or desires, then the all too familiar chain reaction will start all over again: *Do I really want this? Am I only doing this because he/she wants me to do it? Is it my needs, or theirs? Am I letting them walk all over me? Am I being manipulated? Where am I? Who am I? What do I want? Ah! If only I had more self-confidence, then...!*

It can be easy to think this way because *yes*, someone with a high level of self-confidence and self-esteem wouldn't allow him/herself to be exploited, don't you agree?

But it is a long and arduous process which starts with you letting go, taking a step back and out of the situation and learning not to assume or try to figure it out, but just to *be* and *feel* what it is *you* actually want! This requires that you begin trusting yourself and start *believing* in yourself! Be honest to yourself and in your approach towards others!

It's a bit like the story of the man who sits himself down in front of the stove and commands: *Give me fire and warmth, then I'll give you firewood!*

The reality is it works the other way around.

First of all you have to work on believing in and trusting in yourself, your needs, your rights, and your possibilities!

Then work at being honest with yourself and with others and stop trying to figure things out and making assumptions!

The clearer and bolder you are, not only to yourself but also towards others, the more you will grow and the more your self-esteem will increase and you will enter into a healthy and invigorating process, which will subsequently heighten your self-confidence and self-awareness.

You will begin to see and believe the fact that you are the amazing and unique person that you really are because there *IS* only one like you in the whole wide world and you are most definitely unique!

We see, hear and perceive things in a way to make them fit into our vision, our self–perception, our experiences, previous encounters and our "reality", for better or for worse! Remember that there are *always* two sides to the same story. Everybody has their own perspective and one might be just as correct as the other! It is just looking at it in different ways!

When you trust yourself and your values, when you are honest and believe in yourself, when you love yourself as the most amazing person *you* are, then you are living more fully and more completely. You are living *your* life! Then you cannot be rattled, you will not let others' attitudes or opinions control your life, and you will understand and respect the differences.

It all begins with the first step!

Take *RESPONSIBILITY* and resume control over *your* life.   (*See Chapter 6*)

Many of us have had the need to "borrow" others' eyes and others' faith in us because when you set out, our vision will be limited to only being capable of perceiving what we ourselves believe in, based upon the reality we have created about ourselves and our possibilities!

It can be difficult to see yourself as better than you are accustomed to and this can be devastating for your development and the path in your life ahead!

Allow others to help you to see that which you cannot quite yet see. Find someone who has been there themselves, someone you can trust and who only wants the best for you and decide that you *want* to move on, *no matter what*, all the way until you have reached your goal.

Boundaries will have to be crossed and you will have to expand your comfort zone! This is the *only* way to move forward and develop! Each time you cross a boundary, or solve a task, that on the face of it is far from what you thought possible (as viewed from your *earlier* perspective), the more you will grow as a person and the stronger and more proud of yourself you'll become!

If you learn to accept every challenge as a learning process and an opportunity to grow as a person, then you will learn to relish seeking out these challenges, even though they may seem tough and *totally* insurmountable, as if you were standing on the edge of the abyss, without a parachute or a safety net.

Anybody who has gone through deep crises, adversities and defeats *knows* that in the end they have only made them stronger! This mainly applies to people who *want* to change and who manage to take responsibility for their own lives and actions because if you choose to remain a "victim", then growth is impossible! Then you and your life will remain the same!

When you meet someone with success, peace and contentment in their life, it will *always* be someone who has experienced adversity, setbacks and possibly even losses, who is now able to stand even taller and in deeper harmony with him/herself!

You have to yearn for it, *want the change,* because it will not come by itself! But, when it comes down to it, the only thing it really takes is a *decision*!

Then, of course *COURAGE, STRENGTH,* and *PERSEVERENCE!*

BELIEVE ME … IT IS WORTH EVERY SINGLE MOMENT!

Personal notes and comments:

CHAPTER 5

YOU ARE AND RECEIVE WHAT YOU ARE THINKING ABOUT!

You *choose to* see whatever you perceive to be real and that is based upon how you view *your* reality! Even if it is miles away from the "truth", the proper reality, your perception and your view of it, may be the only valid one for you! You are able to create "evidence", to convince yourself, which supports your views and perceptions of things. This is far from being something new. Throughout man's existence, we have lived according to what our "reality" looked like.

We have made decisions, lived, raised families, traded, travelled, etc. We have based our view of life on our perception of reality! Although it may sound strange, maybe even incomprehensible, just think about the times, when people thought that the world was flat!

Wasn't it that everyone lived and made their decisions exclusively based upon this perception of reality? How was it with the first ones who tried to say that the world was round? How were they perceived? Many were proclaimed as insane; some were even burned at the stake for heresy!

A good many of us are living in our own little "flat world" and we have built our lives, thoughts and behavioural patterns to correspond to this reality! If anyone tries to tell us that things are entirely different, for example, that our vision of ourselves and our abilities are totally distorted and have nothing to do with reality, will we not react in a similar way to the people who once attacked those who tried proclaiming that the world was indeed round?

We all present our own arguments and "evidence". We bring out the "big guns", if we feel our lives, or our identities, are being threatened!

Why is this *so* dangerous?

It's due to the fact that we don't know any better!

It is the world we have created, this vision of ourselves, which equates with what we've heard since childhood, and which has become so deeply ingrained inside of us and has turned out to be the absolute truth about us!

It might be a totally innocuous or innocent remark from our parents, siblings, friends, colleagues, or others, which we unconditionally or in a moment of weakness have taken in, and have accepted as the truth! It could be a sibling making fun of the way you eat and, suddenly, it sticks in your head that you have a strange way of eating, and then you get a complex about it when you are eating with others, which makes it even more awkward and then you convince yourself that it *is* true, that you *do* look weird when you eat! You become so embarrassed when you are eating that you are compelled to cover your mouth with your hand and it may even result in you not liking to eat at all, when others are present!

Or it might be your way of walking that was commented upon, or ridiculed at school! Haven't you ever experienced being conscious of the way you walk and felt how stiff and even more awkward it became when you thought hard about it.

Small "innocent" jibes like these, eventually may well influence your self-esteem, your "reality", your choices and thereby your entire life!

Most of us are familiar with these types of incidents! Most of us have experienced it. But it is *how we deal* with these experiences that determine whether they influence our thoughts and actions and consequently our lives. It could just as well be all the things that are left unspoken, all the things that a child might sense, but which are not being said directly and which thereby become confusing to the child. You will often find the child trying to find a reason or an explanation in the physical world for what it senses.

If, for example, the child experiences that its parents are always angry and irritated, that they are constantly arguing and sometimes even end up getting divorced, and if the parents can't manage to make it crystal clear that it has *nothing* to do with the child, then automatically the child will blame itself – because there must be a reason for its parents to separate: *It's more than likely me, my fault! It's probably because I'm difficult, stupid, ugly, fat...!* If the child is not corrected in this impression, it will become the reality the child finds itself in!

For the rest of the child's life it will live by this "reality" and because of that, create situations in keeping with this distorted vision of itself and convince itself to this perception of it being worthless, no good at anything, stupid, fat, ugly, etc! This striving for something physical to relate to as being the cause is very common; it is probably mostly among women that we find this expressed in a negative vision of themselves, very often in a negative view of their own bodies.

Probably many women are familiar with the situation of standing in front of the mirror and seeing something entirely different from what others see – only focusing on their "flaws", just noticing the flab, the too small or too large breasts, the too broad or too flat behind, or of only letting the bathroom scales dictate their mood and thereby what the rest of the day is going to be like, etc.

For the women in question, doesn't it get even worse, this critical and self-destructive vision of ourselves, when everything around us is chaotic?

If, on the other hand, we are on top of the situation and are experiencing success and prosperity, or *decide* to have a positive attitude, don't we then automatically feel even more attractive and more powerful and forget everything about the scales and the flab?

Then we can really take on the world!

It is from your thoughts that you create your world. It is basically your thoughts about yourself that form the foundation for most of your thoughts and actions. Remember, they are your own choices (either consciously or subconsciously). It is a self-reinforcing process, whereby you constantly create situations that confirm your impression of yourself, both the good and positive as well as the bad and negative!

It may be difficult to understand and not least to accept, that you are what you think and that you personally have created and are creating the life you are living and the situations you find yourself in because who would voluntarily place themselves in such difficult, restricting and hopeless situations, which many of us have wound up in? (*See Chapter 2*)

We must remember that it's not at the conscious level that a deliberate thought such as *now I will ruin my life, my relationships, my career* emerges, but that it is because of the pre-conceived ideas we have about ourselves, which affect our behavioural patterns and create this reality!

The only way we can break this vicious cycle is by altering and analysing our thoughts about ourselves and our reality.

It takes strength and perseverance because our subconscious

will fight us tooth and nail! The vision you have created of yourself and your possibilities, is the only one you know and all of a sudden you have to relate to an entirely different truth! See the possibilities; see "the world as round"!

Many people are thinking about and planning their holidays in minute detail, but if you look at their daily lives, it is entirely different! Here things are often left to chance and people are easily swayed or blown off course!

If you don't know where you are heading, you will be easy prey in the game of chance! It is difficult to stay the course and to steer towards a goal that doesn't exist. When you have been sidetracked in your life, how can you return to the right course and get back on track, if you don't know which path to take, or in which direction "the goal" actually is?

There are several clichés and proverbs to verify this!

We all know about "the way of nature", the changing of the seasons, the cycle of life, etc. We can nod in agreement at the very visible and natural processes that are expressed in proverbs like, for example, *You reap what you sow!*

Yes, we can relate to that. How will the farmer be able to harvest anything, if he hasn't planted the seeds in the spring? What will there be to harvest, if he has not tended, nurtured and watered the crops throughout the summer? How large a yield would he harvest, if he just threw the seeds at random, or on soil which had not been cultivated and made ready for planting? Suppose he only throws seeds on stony ground, how large a yield would he obtain then?

It is precisely the same thing with your thoughts – your "seeds"!

How will you be able to harvest the fruits of life, harvest a healthy, productive, contented, successful and richer life, if you are not sowing the right seeds – the right thoughts?

Our brain, our conscious and our subconscious mind, is like a garden or a large field. Anything you plant (accept) in your conscious mind will in due time, through the unconscious mind (our subconscious), manifest itself as a physical "harvest"!

Every thought that we in our conscious mind accept as true or right (as defined by *our* perception of reality, be it true or false), will unfiltered enter into our subconscious, whose sole purpose is to manifest our thoughts. It has no free-will; it cannot distinguish good from bad. Everything we think and accept as the truth, the subconscious will endeavour to make it materialise!

There is no getting around it; good thoughts produce good/positive "crops", whilst bad/negative thoughts produce bad/negative "crops"!

You are what you think. You get or receive what you think! If you *really* understand this, it will be the most extraordinary realisation and at the same time the most "mind blowing" discovery you can have! The day you *really* understand the meaning of "the way of nature" and start living accordingly, you will be able to turn your life around and resume control over it, simply by changing your conscious thoughts!

It is the largest and most powerful discovery and realization you can achieve in your personal development and the world will be at your feet!

Anything you wish for and consciously go after can be yours!

If this is difficult to relate to, then try just for one full day to be consciously aware of your own thoughts, perhaps by writing them down. When the day is over, you will not be surprised about where and why you and your life is where it is today, *be it* for better or for worse!

The more you think about the bad things, the difficult times, the more you'll think about deficiencies and mistakes, the more you are focused on all the negativities, the worse your business will do, the worse your life will be and the more negativity and adversity you will attract! If, on the other hand, you mange to think about abundance, success, and positive experiences then you will attract more of the good things into your life.

Remember proverbs like *You reap what you sow! You've made your own bed, now you have to lie in it!* Suddenly they take on a new and deeper meaning! The vast majority of us will be so entrenched in our habitual thinking, our self-image, our opinion about our possibilities, and our destiny in life, that it will be a too horrifying and provocative truth, so we, instinctively push it to the back of our mind!

Suppress, deny and reject…!

We will be able to then conjure up reams of "evidence" from *our* reality, as to why it isn't true and why it isn't possible, why we are just victims of circumstance!

We feel threatened through our self–awareness, our perception of reality and our "the earth is flat – view" of life.

Only the few who *choose* to embrace that truth and to implement it into their lives and into their world will be able to steer towards, create and live the most amazing life, full of happiness, contentment, positivity, love, abundance and success and enjoy life's bounties, which in reality are accessible to all! They will also reap what they sow and that will ultimately lead to more success and prosperity!

~

Far too many allow what they have here and now, to control or stop them, instead of believing in and going after what they truly desire for their future.

Benedicte Frölich

Personal notes and comments:

CHAPTER 6

TAKE RESPONSIBILITY!

What does it mean to take responsibility?

We all know that we can be held accountable for our actions and behaviour when we become adults! However it's another thing to be responsible towards the rules and regulations of society.

What about the responsibility for your own life and how you choose to live it?

The responsibility for where you are today, and for where you are going to be in the future!

The responsibility for your relationships, for the well being of your family, for you as a parent, for your education, your career and your financial situation, and the responsibility for yourself, your self-esteem and your self-respect!

As long as you abide by the rules and regulations, there isn't really much more for *you* to do, or pay attention to! Everything else, of course, is affected by outside influences, isn't it?

There are the market economy, the job situation, the relationships you're in, your husband or wife, your children, your "here and now" situation – they're all influencing your life!

You think: *What are they going on about, me taking responsibility for my own life? Why, that's what I am doing! I am where I am and have what I have, because...! If only..., then everything would be different! It's not my fault! There is nothing else I can do about it!*

I am sure most of us have either said this, or thought this way at some point in our lives and if we haven't, we certainly know someone who has!

What happened to the life we dreamt about when we were young? The glorious future which looked so bright and promising! The feeling that *all* possibilities were right there lying at our feet!

Now here we are, grown-up and reflecting on the life we ended up with! The financial situation is not quite the one from our dreams, maybe even far from it. Mounting debts, instead of abundance. A job we are probably no longer excited about, but well, it's the one we have! Maybe we find ourselves with a husband or a wife we feel that we don't really know anymore and maybe we can't even remember what it was that we fell for back then!

Whatever happened to love?

Maybe it got ploughed under with the practical chores, the dreary everyday humdrum and stress, with teenage kids accelerating the number of grey hairs and at best one, with maybe two holidays a year, where we can get away from (escape from) the hustle and bustle of day to day life and *finally* be able to live, enjoy, relax, let our hair down and be free of inhibitions.

A week, or maybe two, where we try to recharge our batteries, so that they can last the next 6-12 months in our somewhat dull, dismal and stressed out daily life!

Many scrimp and save for this one (maybe two) week a year, where they can "live", enjoy and let their hair down!

A lot of people, however, have to take loans for this annual "kiss of life", only to be forced to struggle even harder when they return home to be able to pay back the loans which in turn of course leads them to feel even more burned out, to break down even further and to need to get away again even more, to have or get another "fix" (a new holiday) to "fantasy island" far away from the daily grind. It is a never ending spiral that keeps going down, down, deeper and down!

We don't even think about it anymore, because it is simply the way things *are*!

Everybody else is doing the same. That's the way it is!

Life is not supposed to be *easy*; nobody ever said it was!

But the fact is that *you* and *you alone* are responsible for your own life wherever you are in your life, for better or for worse!

THIS is one of the hardest things to accept!

If you are at a stage in your life where it seems bleak, dismal and devoid of any prospects or hope for change, it hurts to hear this! All your defence mechanisms will react, alarm bells will go off in your head and the air will become rife with explanations, recriminations, accusations and anger, because *nobody* voluntarily or consciously *wants* to create a life for themselves that is inferior to the one which they dreamt of when they were young!

 No, it is everybody and everything else which is to blame; it is the economy, it is the society, it is the husband or the wife, the children, the parents. It is the job, the boss, the wealthy, etc.

It's entirely their fault!

What if it's all true - that the cause is down to you? That it *is* your "fault"? That it is your thoughts, your behavioural patterns that have brought you to where you are today? (*See Chapter 5*)

Instead of regarding it as a disaster and instead of blaming yourself for what you *have* done and which anyway cannot be changed, try looking at this knowledge as being the most amazing piece of "news" and as the means to being able to change your life into something better from this day onwards!

Because if you have been able to create this situation, if, as I've said, your thoughts and actions have brought you to where you are today, that will imply that by *changing* your thoughts and behavioural patterns you are also able to change your situation, thus giving you the possibility of creating precisely the life you have always dreamt of; a dream which at some stage in your life you have given up on, given up striving for – and maybe even worst of all – totally given up believing in and dreaming about!

It can simply be too painful to dream of change, because one's situation might seem so hopeless and totally without the possibility of change because once we stop hoping and dreaming, then there isn't much left to go after and when we give up then we have lost *for certain!*

When you have learnt and experienced that it *is* possible to create the life you have always dreamt of, that it *is* possible to be happy and full of contentment *every* day, because it is something that you choose, not something dictated by circumstance, there lies a new beginning for you.

When you, just as I, have walked the path and learnt from and followed in the footsteps of those who *have* succeeded, then it is quite sad to observe how many actually choose to give up, some of them even *before* the first real challenge, and submit to a life of mediocrity and to believe that this is what is in store for them in life!

Especially, when the ones you see doing it are those who are close to you, the ones you really care about!

It *is* tough, at times very tough accepting the challenges and struggles, which must be fought, if you want to create a better life for yourself and your family!

There are many times where we can have wished for someone to appear and relieve us of our burdens, fight our fights and carry us all the way through it, days when the challenges are so daunting and so bewildering that you just feel like hiding under the covers and staying in bed until it has all blown over!

But challenges will keep on occurring until you face them, look them in the eye and learn the lesson that is *always* "hidden" in them!

It is obvious that if we deal with these challenges, the resistance and the adversity that we encounter in our lives, and *choose* to move forward, *choose* to learn from them, and *choose* to see the possibilities rather than the problems that will make us grow and become a stronger person!

Understand that there is *no* development and growth, in either an over protected or an easy life devoid of problems!

There are certainly none who have achieved success in any one area of their lives, who have not also had to face struggles and overcome adversities and challenges! Contrary to what some might think, the challenges do not simply disappear when you are experiencing success and earning a lot of money! It is actually quite the opposite!

The big difference between those who have achieved success and those who have given up, abandoned the hope that it *can* be different, is that those who are successful have learnt that it is *they* who are in control of their lives and therefore are also in control of how they will respond to possible adversities and overcome challenges.

Those who have not understood this unique possibility of being able to create their own lives and their own successes still choose to react to the problems and allow their moods and their daily lives to be governed by this!

They allow their "here and now" situation to dictate the mood they're in. They are victims of their own thought processes. Look at their responses: *Oh, poor me! My financial situation, my job or lack of job! It's because...! It's all the others!*

Plus the excessively used, *If only....!*

I *know* this, because I have been there myself!

I have *lived* it, *thought* it and *believed* it!

It isn't difficult to find legitimate reasons for the problems in one's life. Reasons, excuses and explanations, when repeated enough times to oneself or to others (who are willing to endure them), eventually become the truth or the reality and thereby justify one's negative perception such as: *Poor me! After all, I don't have any influence over my life, or my future!*

Try reminding yourself when you are feeling down and troubled, that from the moment you decide to pick up the gauntlet, it is only a question of time before you will begin to see and feel the results of your efforts!

It is not necessarily something which you will see straight away. Understand though, that even the minutest movement in the right direction will create a change in your current situation and you will certainly progress further with your possibilities of creating the most amazing life and develop into a person you can be proud of! Your self-esteem will grow!

We humans are the only species who have this totally unique capacity, namely, the capacity to choose *and* change! Leland Val Van De Wall writes in *"You Were Born To Choose"*: *When a person takes responsibility for their life and the results they are obtaining, they will cease to blame others as the cause of their results. Since you cannot change other people, blame is inappropriate!*

By blaming others you will confine yourself inside a "mental prison" of your own making.

When *you* take the responsibility for your own life and the casting of blame and accusations ceases, then you will be free to grow and develop!

In ignorance of their possibilities many create this "mental prison" around themselves and their lives, and as Vernon Howard wrote: *You can't escape from a prison, if you don't know you're in one!*

Only a very few people have understood and taken on the responsibility for *all* aspects of their lives!

The men and women for whom you have the greatest respect will probably be those who *have* accepted and *have* taken responsibility for everything, which has happened and is still happening in all aspects of their lives! They also determine how much money they will have to earn to be able to live the life they want, and if it requires more money to achieve other things they might desire, then they will go out and earn it! They will never allow another person's attitudes or opinions to affect them, or determine how they should feel and how they should live their life, no matter what!

They manage and secure for themselves a meaningful vocation, one that stimulates them. They know that it is important how they choose to spend their day and they refrain from engaging in trivial and pointless activities. They travel and are interested in how other people in other cultures live and how they perceive their lives. They have both exciting and stimulating social lives and they are acquainted with likeminded people! You will only rarely, if ever, see these people denounce the responsibility for any unfavourable act or outcome, by putting the blame on others for whatever has transpired!

Whenever a negative situation arises in their lives, they "take it in their stride" because they know and acknowledge that it is themselves who have attracted this negative situation. They know that *everything* has a reason! They learn their lesson and continue scouting for and reaching out for new challenges, new developments and growth!

Back in 1903 Wallace D. Wattles wrote in his book "*The Science of Being Great*": *You become great by doing little things in a great way every day*!

It is precisely these "little" daily activities that make an enormous difference as to whether you will be successful, or remain where you are! You must understand that it is *your* responsibility to do the very best you can in any given situation! Without stepping up and taking responsibility for everything in your life, you will never be able to create the life you wish for!

Winston Churchill said it precisely and succinctly: *Responsibility is the price of greatness!*

Bob Proctor continues: *What many people fail to understand, unfortunately, is that every time we fail to take responsibility, we rob ourselves of the possibility of success!*

We may attempt to avoid taking responsibility, but we will *never* be able to avoid seeing and experiencing the results from it!

Since we can't turn time back, neither to yesterday nor to last year, we cannot change things that *have* happened! We can choose to learn from what has happened and use that and the knowledge we have acquired because of it, to create a different and better future for ourselves and our families!

But much too often we end up wasting time blaming others and complaining, *I should have done this, that and the other!* But whatever you did, or didn't do in the past, will forever remain done/undone!

It can't be changed, just as you can't change, for example, what time you got up this morning!

You did whatever you could with the knowledge and experience you had at *that* precise moment.

On reflection, if you now do not think that you did what you should have done, or ought to have done, then you just have to forgive yourself and move on!

I know from personal experience that this can be very hard to swallow, very difficult to relate to!

If throughout your entire upbringing, you, like me, have only seen, learned and listened to complaints, self-recriminations and guilt, like *You should have known better! Come on, you could have done...! You know very well, that we always...!,* Then you might want to bash yourself over the head with a hammer: *Oh! If only I had done or said it differently, because, really, I should have known better!*

But *NO, NO* and yet again *NO!* This is not how things are!

If you *had* been able to do it differently, then you *would* have done it differently!

Neither you nor anybody else can undo what has happened. All we can do is *learn* from it and you will have to come to terms with this, to be able to move on. It will do you no good to start blaming yourself or others, or to pull out the big hammer and start bashing yourself over the head with it! You should instead try to accept that you did the best you could because that's just how it is; so try to forgive yourself and move on!

Being able to forgive yourself, as well as others, is one of the most important keys to achieving success and making progress in your life. It is important to understand that until we have learnt how to forgive, we will not have sufficient mental strength and the self confidence to live in a responsible manner.

When somebody has not learnt to forgive (themselves as well as others), then naturally these strong and destructive emotions follow suit, namely guilt, regret and anger! By having these domineering and destructive emotions in our minds, there won't be any room for taking responsibility nor for being responsible!

You cannot blame others and take responsibility at the same time!

Putting the blame on others and being responsible by taking on responsibility do not walk hand in hand!

George Bernard Shaw said: *People are always blaming their circumstances for what they are! I don't believe in circumstances! The people, who get on in this world, are the people who get up and look for the circumstances they want and if they can't find them, they make them!*

Bob Proctor adds: *Losers blame and accuse; they don't know that they have the possibility of creating their own opportunities and circumstances! Winners are accountable! Blame and accusation are not words in their vocabulary, nor are they a part of their lives! If things are not quite going according to plan, they create new ideas and possibly they will take a different course and seek new possibilities, which are better suited to their plans!*

The winners' choice *is* to take responsibility for everything which has happened in his/her life, good as well as not so good, because they regard everything that happens as a learning process and therefore always see the good in any situation, even in those that on the face of it are bad and negative!

Therefore: *First* you must recognise your own situation (you must know where you are at right now, i.e., from where you are setting out!), and *then* understand and accept the fact that you yourself have created the situation (with your thoughts and actions throughout the years). *Then* you can begin taking responsibility for your own life and take the first steps towards creating the life you really want!

Remember it all begins with the first step!

With each step you will be coming ever closer to your goals. That in itself is so motivating, when you begin to see, feel and experience the changes in your daily life!

You are unique, simply because of the fact that you *are* and that you can choose and change your thoughts! Thoughts are the foundations for everything. Any outcome in life has its origin in thought! Your thoughts are your own and because of this, you are unique and capable of creating the life and the situations which *you* want! Or, to put it another way, *Your life is created from your thoughts!*

When people deny their responsibility, they are putting their life, their present situation, into the hands of other people and will no longer have any control over their own future!

People who do this can do no more than wait (anxiously) for whatever tomorrow, next week and next year may bring! They can only hope for something good to happen. But given previous situations and experiences, it is far more likely that they will anticipate and fear something which they really do not want to happen!

When you are placing your life into other peoples' hands in this way, you will have to accept whatever comes your way. You are governed by their thoughts, desires and actions and guess what they have planned for you and your life? *Nothing much!*

I have met – and I have previously done it quite often myself – many people using a great deal of money (which they mostly don't even have), on readings and predictions about their future. They have their tarot cards read, they visit fortune-tellers, they have their horoscopes done, they purchase crystals, change their names after having visited numerologists, and so on. Everything was done with the hope of hearing that everything will be different in the future, that something or someone will appear to enchant their lives and make them happy!

But you are the *only* person in the whole wide world who can predict with any measure of accuracy *your* own future! From the very day when you decide to take the responsibility for your own life and for the results you have achieved, you will be free to create *your* life!

Taking this responsibility brings with it a deeper self-confidence and a fortified belief that your dreams and goals really *can* come true!

You will, however, need to know that when you, like the other winners, decide to accept that your insights as well as your thoughts and behavioural patterns are your own responsibility, no matter what your "here and now" situation might be, it is *you* who choose how well you will do!

At the same time you *will* set yourself apart from the greater majority, who still live in compliance with the dictum: *It's all their fault!*

Furthermore, your actions and reactions, not to mention your results, may seem incomprehensible and may in some cases be even deeply provocative to them.

Although everyone around you is naturally wishing the best for you, it is not necessarily the most popular decision to go against the stream – to be different!

Everybody wants development but nobody wants change!

This awareness that you can create your life by taking responsibility for your thoughts and actions is one of the biggest revelations that you can have. One way you can strengthen this and make it penetrate deeper into your subconscious and thereby make it *your* truth, is by saying out loud to yourself: *I am responsible for MY life, MY feelings, MY personal development and ALL the results I get!*

Say it at least 10 times a day, *every day*, for at least 30 days and you will be able to create a highly sensitive awareness of this truth. You will reach the point where blaming someone or something for your situation will cease and you will be ready to grow and move forward in your life!

But remember old thoughts and behavioural patterns die hard and they will not lightly step down in favour of new and "controversial" thoughts. So if your reasons for change are not powerful enough, if it is not an "at any cost" attitude, the old familiar thoughts and behavioural patterns will take control again and they will tell you that all that "stuff" about you being able to create a better life for yourself is utter nonsense! It is precisely like the weeds in your garden: if you don't fight them and keep them away *all the time,* they will grow and spread and eventually dominate the entire garden!

You must understand and accept what kind of "forces of nature" you are up against and on a daily basis do whatever it takes to keep your mind, or your "garden" the way you want it to be, now and in the future!

Your mental "weeds" are all the controlling voices and your self-esteem, what you *think* you can do and what you think other people think about you and your abilities! If you allow other people to dictate what you can, may, or will, then in reality you are allowing them to "infest" *your* "garden"!

You are probably all too familiar with these persuasive voices and thoughts, which confine you to where you already are! After all, that which we already have, which we are most familiar with, is a safe and secure place to be – no matter how much we might be suffering, or restricted in our growth.

It is this same security and particularly her lack of self-esteem, which again and again makes the battered woman return to her violent husband. You may hear her say: *NOW it is going to be different. Now he will change; he promised!*

Fortunately it is but a minority (although still far too many) who live in such relationships, which often lead to frustration, a feeling of helplessness, as well as anger, even in those who witness it!

But, is it not precisely the same thing that we are doing, when we choose to remain in the life we are living (governed by outside influences and other peoples' whims), rather than going after our own dreams?

It is equally hard for those who really love you to watch you give up on your dreams and live a life following other peoples' rule books and desires. Watch you withering away, "squandering" your unique abilities and talents and discarding your own possibilities for an amazing life!

This is not physical violence with visible injuries! No, this is the psychological violence you are allowing yourself to be exposed to by not taking the responsibility for your life!

This kind of "abuse" is very often much more difficult to handle because we are (and often for far too long) capable of convincing ourselves as well others that: *I am doing ok! There is nothing wrong with me, many other people are far worse off than me! It will pass! Maybe someday...!* (Which everybody knows will never come)!

This is the mental prison I mentioned earlier because once again, how can you escape from a prison that you don't even know exists, or which you adamantly deny the existence of?

One very important aspect of taking responsibility and being responsible lies in the difference between being responsible *on behalf of* and being responsible *for!*

You are responsible for *your* feelings and *your* results, not on behalf of anybody else's!

You might possibly have assumed the responsibility *on behalf of* somebody else but not *for* somebody else (except of course, when you have children, who have not yet come of age).

Often it becomes easy, thinking that somebody else will take the responsibility and carry the burden, when we find it just *too* heavy to carry, *too* complicated or *too* painful. We can easily convince ourselves that it would make it much easier for us and set us free, that we would be able to live more relaxed and carefree. If we do not stop right there and think this idea to its logical conclusion, we will not see that the outcome will be the exact opposite!

When we allow other people to assume responsibility for our lives, we become dependent upon them! They become the "givers" and we become the "receivers". Our well-being now becomes totally dependent on their generosity or charity! In this way it can be very easy to create much confusion, frustration and limitations in life, *both* for the "giver" as well as for the "receiver".

Nothing good will ever come from this type of situation! When you assume responsibility for somebody else's feelings and results (only to help them, of course), you will break down and destroy their self-confidence and self-respect!

Most people are going through life with their focus on receiving, convinced that it is the others that should provide and care for us! They will automatically expect this and accept this, but, on the other hand, they will not appreciate the "givers", because in this way an unequal relationship between them has been established. They will come to feel obliged to the "givers", who in turn will feel that the "receivers" now owe them something and in the very least should show some gratitude and respect. Furthermore, the "receiver" will instinctively feel that the "giver" is preventing them from learning to take care of themselves and this makes for feelings of inferiority and resentment towards the "giver"!

If the "giver" is not aware of this fact, he/she will naturally become confused, angry and even hurt.

You may even hear them (as well as maybe yourself) say: *Why don't they like me, after everything I have done for them?*

When you assume somebody else's responsibilities and you are doing what they themselves should have done (even when this is done with the best of intentions and only to help them, since they are in *such* a difficult spot), you contribute to keeping them stuck in a rut, with no possibility of learning from and growing with their challenges. This way you contribute to breaking down their self-confidence and their self-respect too!

Since most people are always seeking the easy way out and reject or avoid taking responsibility, they will automatically expect you to do more and more for them!

An Italian proverb goes like this: *He who allows a goat to be placed on his shoulders will soon be forced to carry a cow!*

On the other hand, it is your duty to help people become conscious of their own responsibilities and the advantages of choosing to take on these responsibilities! When you allow somebody else to take on *your* responsibilities, you place yourself in a prison, where eventually deficiencies, limitations, accusations and an unfulfilling life will inevitably emerge!

The awareness and importance of taking responsibility and being responsible for your own life, for your own feelings and for every result achieved, is something that should be taught to you during childhood, but as this rarely happens, most people slide ever deeper into a kind of "welfare mentality" (it is the others, who should provide and I should receive!) and they abandon all responsibilities and live a life accusing and blaming everyone!

Where there is an absence of responsibility, there is an absence of self respect!

Once you understand and take on the responsibility for your own life, you will naturally stop your accusations against other people. Then, when guilt and blame have been eliminated from your life, you will be *free* to develop and become a stronger person, with a high level of self-respect and a strong conscience and you will be able to develop the most amazing life!

Remember, we can't change other people; we can *only* change ourselves!

It all begins with *you* taking responsibility for yourself!

THERE IS A RESPONSIBILITY TO BE TAKEN – AND A LIFE TO BE LIVED!

Personal notes and comments:

CHAPTER 7

COURAGE

What does it mean to be courageous? When we think about a courageous person, many of us think of physical acts because it is much easier to relate to something physical, something we can see, touch and measure, rather than to a courageous act on the humane or personal level!

YES! It does take courage to throw yourself out of a plane at 3,000 metres altitude and plunge 1,000 metres in free fall, before the parachute opens, but it takes just as much, if not more, to step out beyond your comfort zone and change something in your life!

Is it not courageous to dare to go beyond the safe and the familiar, to dare to plunge into uncharted and deep waters?

Wanting to change your present situation requires courage; it requires taking a decision about wanting something different – something more!

The bottom line is that courage is about taking a decision! But how do you measure courage? How do you figure out how much courage will be needed to change your life and to pursue your goals and dreams, and to break the boundaries and do away with prejudices and the 'what we are used to doing' mentality!

There are actually *so* few who really do it, who *dare* to go against the flow, *dare* to stand out from the crowd, and *dare* to believe in themselves and in their dreams!

You run the risk that your family and friends will turn their backs on you because when you pursue your dreams you are actually a "threat", at least on the subconscious level, to those who remain behind!

They will notice your changes and see you as the "strange" one, one who chooses to leave the community, the social climber, or "ass kisser", to put it more negatively, who ingratiates himself or herself with the boss, or the superiors just to get promoted. (There is actually very rare focus on the fact that this might well be an aspiring person, who is actually doing a very good job, working hard and doing whatever it takes to reach his/her goals, a promotion, for example!).

Ask yourself honestly, haven't we all at some point in our lives joined the crowd, joined in with the demeaning and the "back stabbing" of someone, because we thought that they were changing too much? Blindly followed suit in the slandering, *without* stopping to find out what was actually behind this person's aspirations or change. Because if we are all in the same boat, all fed up with the same things, or having the same problems to complain about, then nobody is any better off than anybody else, and we can all group together in our "community" of moaning and complaining.

Courageous is the one who *dares* to go against the "community", the one who wants change and who will therefore no longer settle for, or accept, things the way they are!

The truth which only too few *really* understand is that to get something different, you will have to do something different, from what you are used to doing!

If you do what you are used to, you will get what you are used to!

To get more out of life, you will have to develop more! If you don't begin to think and act differently, you will continue to get what you have always been getting and live the way you have always been living!

If you decide to go after that which *you* want, if you decide to change what *you* are unhappy about (and surely the rest are also unhappy or dissatisfied about it), you run the risk that they will turn their backs on you, because from their point of view, it is you who are the "traitor", who deserts them!

What do you have in common with them, now that you have changed what you were unhappy about, or now that you have achieved your goal?

It could arise out of small and rather trivial things, as, for example, you deciding that you want to lose weight! It could be something which you and your colleagues have been talking about for a long time; maybe you all *would like* to lose weight and several times have proclaimed: *NOW is the time! NOW we are going to do it!* But time and again everybody backs out and it never gets beyond the talking and the many half-hearted attempts!

If, however, you are resilient, remain steadfast and achieve your goal, *you* succeed and now there you are: slimmer, looking good and very proud. What happens then? Many will probably say: *wow, that's great, well done!* But deep down they will feel that you have betrayed them because when you are successful, it becomes even more obvious to everybody else that *they* are the "losers", who are still left behind with their weight problems!

Now you have very little in common to talk about and to be together about, because you've already achieved your goal!

One thing is that they might turn their backs on you; another is that you will also probably look for other contacts, because at the same time, you will have moved on so much in your development that *you* just can't stomach listening to all their explanations and excuses for why they failed to follow through again. Now you *know*, that it is *"just"* a question of taking a decision and then sticking with it! If you can, then so can they!

Far too many people are tying themselves down in bad and sometimes even damaging relationships and situations, for the very reason that they don't have the courage to break away!

But for whose sake are you "hanging around"? Nobody will thank you, if you, for example, remain in a poor relationship or a lousy job situation, or give up on a weight loss project, when you end up with stress, develop cardio-vascular diseases, or diabetes!

This may be pushing it a bit! Or is it? *What* is the best for you? What is it worth, living your life, taking care of yourself and going after your dreams and goals? You are the only one who can take care of yourself (and I don't mean only in a physical sense), and you will have to be serious about that!

You can be much more for others and help others even better if you are alive and doing well!

When will you start living *your* life? What does it take and who determines the criteria for what is good for you?

I once knew a head surgeon, who for many years had been building on his dream – a big boat! His goal was to build it himself and sail around the world together with his family. His family and friends went along with it and were very supportive. Everybody was talking about goals and dreams and let themselves be swept along with it, because it was *only* fantasy and yet everybody could still join in!

But then one day the boat was ready and the head surgeon had made his dream come true! He and his wife sold their house, resigned from their good, secure jobs and ventured out on the high seas with their children – to live their dream!

Remaining behind were now the family and friends, who were now confronted with the fact that here was somebody, who really did what they were all talking about! Somebody, who had had the courage to pursue his dreams and to do something about what he was not content with in his life took the decision and followed it through!

At this stage our subconscious will automatically take over again and it will fight tooth and nail against the "threatening" changes because what is happening may be so far outside our comfort zone that it takes courage just to try to understand it. But it will be even more over-stepping our limits to actually do something about it!

It will be difficult to admit to not having had the courage oneself to pursue one's dreams, and for this reason, as I've previously said, the focus shifts towards the one, or the ones, who are changing!

Then, the gossip really got going, fingers were pointed and contempt expressed when the head surgeon "just" sailed off into the distance.

In the end almost everybody turned their backs on the family and continued with their lives as before, except for the one difference, that now they all totally agreed that it's simply not done "just like that". *What about your job, children, family, friends? You have obligations! I can't believe they just left us, the traitors! Egotistical ********!*

They only care about themselves!

It takes *courage* to live your own life, to pursue your dreams because there will always be some (actually many), who will be affected and maybe even provoked by your actions!

Consider for whose sake you are doing whatever it is you have to do, and when you have taken the decision, stick by it, *no matter what!*

It is *this* very act which takes courage!

You could, however, also use other more physical acts and challenges to grow and evolve as a person because the more you throw yourself in at the deep end and overcome some of life's major challenges and crises, the stronger you'll become and then what other people think will be less important to you!

If you observe those who are successful and who have pursued their dreams and goals, you will find, as I've mentioned earlier, that they are all people who have conquered and survived great challenges and who today stand stronger and taller than ever before! They are those who have the courage to get back on their feet, learn from their mistakes and decide to move forward!

Thomas Edison who experienced "failures" so many times in his long research career, chose to look at the many failed experiments, rather as experiments that did *not* work. He utilised his newly acquired experience to throw himself into more new experiments with even greater zest. His attitude was straight forward: *Our greatest weakness lies in giving up! The most certain way to succeed is always to try just one more time!*

You haven't failed until the day you lie down and give up!

We find many people who do not start living their lives on their own terms until, for example, they are diagnosed with a serious, possibly fatal illness, or if they lose a child or a family member, are hit hard financially, and so on, because *then* it is justifiable to opt out. Then it will be more acceptable to one's relations and to the society and also to oneself, apparently!

Why, we might ask ourselves, does it have to be like that?

I will not delay living *my* life, just until a more acceptable reason emerges!

We only have this one life and if we are not going to make the best of it right NOW, then when?

We will of course all meet with new and even bigger challenges that will call for us to show courage time and time again! Mistakenly many wish for fewer challenges and expect that they may live a carefree and quiet life. Believe me, the day the challenges cease to exist, will be the day when life is over, because then you will cease to develop and grow as a person!

As clearly and succinctly as Jim Rohn put it: *Don't wish it was easier; wish you were better! Don't wish for less problems; wish for more skill! Don't wish for less challenges; wish for more wisdom!*

COURAGE is one of the three elements for success. It takes:

COURAGE to acknowledge where you are and what you want, and

COURAGE to go against the flow!

Secondly:

STRENGTH - to act on this knowledge, and last, but not least,

PERSEVERENCE - to continue *until . . .* no matter which challenges you might encounter along the path towards your goal and your reward: A life so much richer on all levels!

It all begins with you "just" taking a decision!

BELIEVE ME, IT IS WELL WORTH IT!

Personal notes and comments:

CHAPTER 8

HOPELESSNESS/HOPE

At which point is your situation or your life hopeless? When and how are you going to find the courage and the hope to move forward?

What controls your life? What is it that *you* allow to "disturb" and create the feeling of hopelessness that you find yourself in? Often our present situation can totally paralyse us and make us feel that we are so "up to our necks in it" or that the "hole" we are in is so deep that we can't "dig ourselves out of it." Or it may be that there is *no* hope for us, or for our future!

Far too many people stand around peering down, their gaze and mind transfixed on the muck *in which they are wallowing around!* That only makes them sink even deeper into it, as if they were standing in quicksand.

Haven't many of us, at one point or another, been there, having been consumed by the hopelessness, loss of courage, motivation but with the hope that at some point things will be different?

It is one thing that we ourselves think it seems hopeless and that we fail to see any way out at all. It is entirely different when, on top of that, someone else, some "well-meaning" person, tells you: *You choose how you want things to be,* while you are in the midst of wallowing in the mire, keeping yourself trapped in the role of a victim!

Whoa! As if it wasn't tough enough already! As if you had voluntarily trapped yourself in this situation!

But there *is* no getting away from it; it is your thoughts and what you are focused on which decides what you will attract into your life! It is you who decide how you choose to react to whatever you have or whatever occurs in your life!

We can't always master what happens in our lives, but we can learn to master how we react to the challenges! Should the challenges, our problems and our "here and now" situations be allowed to determine, which mood we are in? (*See Chapter 5*)

Many people will probably think: *Come on, how can you possibly imagine being content and in a good mood, when everything is falling apart around you?*

Try taking a step back for a moment and look at it from another perspective. Why *shouldn't* you be able to choose to feel good and be content?

Does your situation improve, when you are in a bad mood as well, walking around depressed, angry, mad, irritated, taking it out on your children, your spouse, your colleagues, friends, etc.? Would that change the situation? Or do you think that it actually contributes to keeping you in the mire?

Many experience a brief respite when they take it out on somebody else, because then there are others who also feel lousy! Then the thought, conscious or subconscious is: *If I have to suffer, so do they!*

Many choose to revel at other peoples' misfortunes. Just look at what's on the news, in the papers, and what the gossip columns are overflowing with!

When we see others suffering hardships or losing possessions, we can shift our focus from ourselves onto them and we don't feel quite so alone in our misery, and we say: *Look, there are others who are also having a rough time!*

We prefer to see the rich and the famous having troubles, because then we can convince ourselves that it is no better to be rich and famous, which is a situation so far removed from what we ourselves believe we can achieve. It is so far from our vision of ourselves and our self-perception. If we don't believe that we can, or are allowed to, do something, then the thought arises that nobody else should either.

Isn't there an element of glee when we hear of their problems and misfortunes?

There are some very strange mechanisms which kick in with people "in times of crisis." When we don't believe that we can, when our vision of ourselves is so far from what we see, then our subconscious, with all its different voices and thought patterns, takes over and fights back.

It is true that being in a good mood can't always change a situation right away and all the bad won't turn into good merely by snapping our fingers, but it *will* help you to move forward, if you choose to be content and constantly try to maintain focus on your goals and dreams, to look towards what you wish your ideal life to be like!

So why not decide to be content, rather than angry and dejected? Isn't it much more enjoyable to be content? Isn't it much more pleasant to be together with contented and positive people, rather than sour, sulky, whining, moaning and complaining people?

If you don't take the decision that now *enough is enough*, then everything will remain the same, as it was before! You know, if we continue doing what we have always done, we will continue to receive what we have always received! (*See Chapter 7*)

Actually it is a boon to have these challenges and from time to time to be in these hopeless and difficult situations! If they can bring you to a point in your life where you say: *Enough is enough,* then, *if* you decide to use it constructively and learn to see *all* situations and challenges as learning processes, well then the fundamental elements have been laid for the creation of a most amazing life!

A life which *you* create, plan and control! A life filled with hope and contentment!

How many times have you noticed – maybe even experienced it yourself – that it is not until they hit the rock bottom that people (finally) make the decision to change their lives? Those who do will rise up and stand tall as incredibly strong, self-confident, proud and successful people!

Very successful and very wealthy people are those who have many times met with and overcome some of life's biggest challenges!

You can ask yourself: What is success? At which point will I have achieved success?

Success has *nothing* to do with how many material things you might have amassed! It is from the very moment when you take the decision to change your life that you are a success! Far too many people think mistakenly that it is not until they have reached their ultimate target and have achieved what they set out for that they can rightfully claim to be a success. The fact is, however, that it is when you take the decision to set out for your goal that you become a success!

In *that* very moment, hope is created and the gauntlet taken up!

These people are already a success, just by taking a decision.

For *everything* begins with a decision!

You choose your mood, you choose how things or situations around you will influence you!

From the moment you decide that *enough is enough* you become master of your own life!

As certain as the changing of the seasons, you *will* experience Spring, a new beginning following even the harshest and longest of Winters!

It is always *when things seem darkest that you are the closest*; always remember this!

This is where perseverance comes into the picture. If you keep at it for long enough, it is a law of nature that you will progress in your life and achieve your goals!

Over time there have been countless stories bearing witness to this lesson, that the one who perseveres, who keeps fighting for and believing in it, will invariably reach the reward. Far too many, unfortunately, give up at the slightest sign of resistance; others capitulate when things are at the toughest and most difficult phase! But it is exactly at *this* very point that one should stand one's ground and fight on! You must remind yourself that after all your tribulations, there are new and brighter times ahead and that it is when things seem darkest that you are the closest.

Take the decision that it will be *you* controlling your life! Don't leave it to chance! Your life is far too valuable for that! Do not let luck or chance dictate how far you will reach, or what you will achieve in your life!

It will do no good to just sit around hoping. Many live their lives hoping to win in the lottery and the only active effort needed for that is to buy a ticket week after week.

There are just as many who live in the hope of the big win, but who don't even buy a lottery ticket! This is where all reason grinds to a halt! How can you win *without* a ticket; how can you score *without* a goal?

Will your life fall victim to the game of chance?

Would you, for example, let something as important as your child's birthday party be open to chance? – *All right, honey, let's see if anybody shows up! Maybe someone has baked a cake! Maybe some people are aware that it is your birthday today and they feel like celebrating it with you!*

The thought that anybody would do or say such a thing is ludicrous. But isn't it the same type of thing you are doing to your life by allowing everyone *but* yourself to decide?

When the storms are raging, with nobody at the helm, your boat will be tossed around all over the place! We can't control the winds, we can't control our surroundings. We can *only* learn to set the sails properly, so that we can steer the boat to where we want to go!

Dare to take control, take a firm grip on the helm and use the force of the wind, the challenges of your life, to blow you ahead, rather than allowing yourself to be tossed around on the high seas of hopelessness and chance!

We can't avoid the down troughs, the raging storms of our lives, but we can learn from them! Then the next time a challenge appears, the next time the storms are gathering, we will be better at gauging and reading the winds, so that we can stand stronger and be better prepared!

What many people regard as resistance and as something which will hold us down and destroy our lives, –may actually be that which drives us ahead towards new and better times.

They say that *hope springs eternal*! Can you find anything more life-enhancing than the sight of the first delicate shoots sprouting after a long time of drought, a fierce forest fire, or the severest of winters?

So, in the midst of your despair, shift your gaze from where you are standing, from the mess you feel is reaching up to your nose, and take the decision that you *will* take over the control of your life and enter the fray no matter what!

Remind yourself that when it seems the darkest, you are the closest!

You have nothing to lose, yet everything to win!

WHICH IS OF COURSE A MOST AMAZING LIFE!

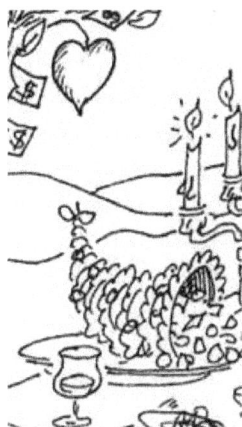

~

Personal notes and comments:

CHAPTER 9

LIVING IN THE EXTREMES

ALL or NOTHING, EITHER /OR, BLACK or WHITE, YES or NO, RIGHT or WRONG. This is the way many of us are spending our lives thinking and acting!

Many of us are allowing our lives and decisions to be ruled by whether we *think* we can handle the tasks or challenges we are confronted with. What we see, or more frequently what we *think* other people see, as "the perfect end result," tends much too often to be that which we build our decisions on.

We think that if we do not acquire the optimal result, if we do not reach the goal whatever it might be, we will have failed! Then we will feel or be looked upon as being a failure!

So it's much better and much safer to leave it alone and say *No,* from the very start!

When we are asked if we feel like doing it, or if we can handle it, our answers will all too often be based on whether we *think* we can handle it and complete the task to *perfection!*

If you are living in the extremes, there will only be *right and wrong - made it, or didn't make it.*

Most often our answer will be: *Uhm, Maybe! I can try, but...* followed by numerous reservations. We are really beating about the bush there.

Suppose you say: *Yes, I can do that* and then find out that you can't after all. Whoa! Disaster! Am I right?

How can we say YES to something about which we have no idea, whether we can handle it or not, because maybe it is the first time we are facing this particular task or challenge?

Haven't we all been there on public display in our worst nightmare, for example, at school, made the laughing stock and pointed at, because we didn't make it, or because we couldn't complete the task?

More often than not it is those who are a bit too cocky and self confident whom we pick on! Those, who say *Yes, I can do that* and who just throw themselves into it, first time, or not.

The Tall Poppy syndrome, the hubris/nemesis way of thinking, kicks in, with the voices booming: *Don't go believing that you are better than us!*

If they fail to succeed, or have to give up, then the rest just stand there only focusing on the fact that they did *not* succeed!

We tend to forget that this person actually tried his/her utmost! Isn't our reaction really against this self-assuredness, whilst we neither had the self-confidence, nor their tenacious attitude, to "just do it"? Therefore, we feel the need to pick on and belittle them, if it "luckily" fails! Aren't we quietly gloating a little bit that he/she (despite the self- confidence and the devil-may-care attitude) couldn't make it after all?

Isn't it almost equally as provocative when this person just gets back on his/her feet, brushes the dust off and is ready to endeavour out into new and untried challenges again?

How can he/she? He/she just failed to do it right! He/she didn't make it!

But the very thing, which characterises the top leaders and the most successful people, is that they "just do it", that they have this calmness and belief in their own worth and abilities, that they *know* they are always doing their utmost!

Isn't that actually what it is all about, always doing your utmost in any given situation, no matter what other people might think and feel?

Are we a success *only* when *everything* works out?

Are we successful *only if* we achieve the ultimate end result?

Who has the right to decide, when and if it is good enough?

Too many people are living on the premise that they want to see "it" (see the result), *before* they believe in it! But we know full well that it is the other way round. You must believe in it *before* you can see and achieve it!

Many are mentally at the finish line *before* they have even started. But when your mind is otherwise occupied by, for example, worrying about the outcome and what others might think, by whether you can perform well enough, etc., you will not be present in the now, you will not be able to distance yourself from the situation and reflect on what is happening and where you are heading!

You might choose the easy way out, which is of course by saying *NO!*, to withdraw before even trying to avoid possible failure and appear as a failure.

This restricts, inhibits and stops us in our development!

Without even taking a crack at it, we will never get any further, never learn what can or must be learned from the challenges ahead.

This is because *everything* is a process. *Everything* has a beginning and is a process or a development towards a goal!

Isn't it then a bit unrealistic if you try stepping out of the situation and looking at it from the outside, to think that you can go straight from the starting point directly to the finish line, or even be at the finish line already *before* you have even started?

We make assumptions and try to figure it all out! But can we do that in every actual situation?

If it was a mechanical or well-tested process, we can deliberate and compare all the gathered data and assess the consequences and results from the normal chain of events.

But when they are tasks or challenges that we haven't even tried before, we can *only* do our best, judged from where we presently are in our lives, with the experience and knowledge we might have at the time.

We can listen to and gather knowledge from others who have tried something similar but we will always have to go through the process from start to finish and no matter how well we have tried to prepare ourselves, we will still experience unexpected challenges along the way!

Other people can't do it for us either; their experience and advice may not suit our view point, or how we deal with the task!

Have you ever heard the expression, *Life got in the way?*

This is exactly what can happen. We are all human and even though from the beginning we may have the best intentions about reaching the goal, or solving the problem, things may get in the way and prevent us from reaching it, things that knock us off course, things that make us shift our focus and attention away from the task, things that cause us to reassess our priorities, so that the task, which was previously *so* important, suddenly is downgraded, as compared to the crisis, the tragedy, the sickness, etc.

Challenges, whether they are good or bad, positive or negative, will be equally "disturbing"!

Look at a new mother, lovers or newly-weds. Where is their focus?

Should we, therefore, avoid starting up with something new because we can't be 100% sure that we can handle the challenge and reach the goal? Does it *have* to be perfect before it is good enough? What is "perfect" anyway? Should we say *"No, thank you,"* if we are not familiar with the "way", or if we can't see the goal, before we begin?

NO, absolutely not!

When you are living in the extremes, as in, for example, wanting everything to be perfect before it is good enough, you are denying yourself of a lot of experiences and putting yourself and your performance under extreme pressure!

We are judging ourselves and our abilities against unrealistic criteria and demands!

Is it at all possible to achieve "perfection"?

Will it not always be possible to do it just a little bit better?

When it actually never will be good enough (if we are striving for "perfection"), haven't we then failed?

When we fail, aren't we failures as people and as leaders? Are we not running the risk of being ridiculed and of people turning their backs on us?

If mentally you are already at your goal, or are trying to figure out what the end result should be then something will always get in the way, you will always be able to find a reason for why you cannot, why you are not ready, etc.

How can you prepare yourself for something when you have no idea what it is, or will be? You can only do it by trying, by taking the first step!

If you have never learnt to believe in yourself, or listen to your own needs or feelings, but have always tried to figure out what *other* people might want or what they might "expect" from you, what will your answer be, if you are asked what *you* feel like?

When we succumb to what other people might think, when we are scared of not being good enough, or of people turning their backs on us, or of being abandoned (because we are not doing what we think they expect us to do), then we will be much more prone to feeling that we'd rather do what they say and choose to go "all in", now that we have already said YES!

So, although we might feel that it is absolutely not what we thought, and that we really have no desire to continue, then the anxiety of disappointing, causing pain, looking like a failure because we were unable to complete the task, will be so enormous that we press on regardless of the inner voices, screaming at us to stop, that this is wrong, that we really don't want to continue!

In particular, the "nice girls" often have great difficulty drawing the line because they want to please and accommodate and the whole time they have to try and work out the right mode of behaviour, how to be and what to do, to ensure that the others will like them!

Frequently, when you are brought up with "conditional love", which is probably the most effective but also the most damaging form of upbringing, you see these reactions and thought patterns.

It is probably the greatest personal threat to lose your parents' love, with, for example, the "threat" of being abandoned, or being unworthy of affection!

It is shocking, but you often hear the following:

If you don't come right NOW, we'll leave you here! Or: *If you don't do what we say, you're not deserving of our love! Nobody loves you, nobody wants you!*

In this way the child quickly learns to disguise and ignore its own desires and feelings, thinking: *I MUST do as they say, so that they will still love me and not leave me!* This way of thinking can at worst lead to a child or an adult, who is constantly controlled by anxiety of loss, being put in a situation that feels like an actual assault, if they daren't speak out or say no!

We will begin to doubt our own emotions if we time and time again ignore them, and only do what we think others expect of us! There will be a discord between what we feel and what we do, which will eventually lead to a refusal to trust our own feelings and what *we* really want!

You can become so confused about your own needs and desires that the simple question of whether you take coffee or tea will result in your being unable to answer. Your brain will go into overdrive, trying to figure out what the correct response should be! But if you can't gauge your feelings, or if the urge is not strong enough, then you will, to protect yourself, either say *I don't know,* or *No thank you!*

When we are talking about slightly bigger decisions than coffee or tea, this mode of thinking, and your need to accommodate everyone else, can have serious consequences! For example, if the man you met at a party says that he wants to be involved with you, and that he can feel that the feeling is mutual, *Come on! You know you want to!* Your belief that you have to accommodate everyone else to avoid rejection and loss of affection – due to your upbringing – will result in putting you in an awful dilemma, due to the fact that a *YES* for you means *"all the way"*!

What if it isn't what you expected, but even though you really don't want to, you think you have to do it anyway because others expect you to?

Oh no! You've backed yourself into a corner and there is no way out of it!

The more you try to feel, the more desperate it becomes; the more rigid you become, the less you feel and the more you will doubt your feelings, etc. The vicious spiral keeps spiraling downwards!

It eventually ends up with you only being able to say *YES* when you are absolutely certain of what you want, and that you truly feel the urge to do it. If you are unable to feel your emotions and desires because you are very confused and you are trying to work out what is "correct", then for you there is no such thing as *a small desire!*

It is *ALL or NOTHING, EITHER /OR, BLACK or WHITE, YES or NO, RIGHT or WRONG.* Because you've said "A", you now are obliged to say "B"!

It's once again the extremes and perfection you strive for, the totally unobtainable! For you there's no way back if you've started something, or have said YES!

According to your way of thinking you could be held accountable and later be confronted with: *YOU said YES yourself! YOU wanted to do it!*

If you don't have the courage, strength or self-esteem to just tell yourself: *Yes, I know I said YES, but now I can feel that it isn't really what I wanted, so now I'm going to stop and change direction and totally ignore what other people think*, then it can almost become a mortal struggle for you!

But there *isn't* any right or wrong. There are actions and the resulting consequences of these actions! There are many more nuances involved. It's not just black or white! The term "perfect" doesn't exist either, for who is to say what is perfect or when something is perfect?

A little desire is still a desire, but it doesn't categorically mean that you have to go the whole distance! So you can also have a little desire for something and feel curious to want to try and experiment with something new, perhaps even something unknown to you!

You have the freedom to choose, the freedom to take one step at a time *and* to change direction if it is not to your benefit.

Let's take pregnancy as an example. There's conception followed by nine months gestation until you stand there full term and ready for delivery. But you have been pregnant for the whole duration of the nine months, not just the last few weeks before the baby arrives!

A desire can therefore also be a brief "two month" desire, one which you can act on, but can you see the end result, or how it will end up from your present situation? Can you calculate ahead what your situation will be when you are five months along? No you can't! All you can do is take one step at a time!

You can also read everything available about raising toddlers, but it is *only* once you have them in your arms that you can actually, physically begin you relationship with the child. Even then, don't we, with monotonous regularity, continue to experience that things still don't go according to plan?

Normally it goes *completely* wrong when we try to work out what others might think, mean and believe to be "perfect"!

For then we are really out on a limb, and have set ourselves an impossible task, especially when we begin to adjust and live our lives according to what we *believe* others might think, being controlled by the fear of failure, of being abandoned or not being loved anymore!

If we have to try to calculate what is needed for us to be "perfect" in the eyes of others, then we have already succumbed to failure, because you can never second guess what they want!

What something means to you will nearly always have a completely different meaning to someone else!

It is only when we first begin living *our* life, when our self-esteem and self-confidence is high, when we believe in ourselves and know that we *always* do the best we possibly can in any given situation, dependant on where *we* are, that other people's opinions suddenly seem to have no impact or influence on our choices or pursuits!

Once we reach that point we accept that there are only *actions* and consequences of these actions, that there is no right or wrong way, and there is no such thing as "perfect"! That is when we begin to see life's nuances and understand that we and *we alone* are responsible for all our actions, and thereby will have to face the consequences of these actions, be they good or bad! Only then will we become free and independent individuals with the opportunity for growth and development!

Life in all its diversity offers a plethora of possibilities, colours and sensory perceptions lying right there at our feet!

It is only when you cease struggling to predict the end result, only when you release the "extremes" and your endless search for perfection, only then will you be able to enjoy *the present moment!* Not before!

Let go, live life, and decide that you *always* do your utmost in every given situation. Learn from your mistakes and progress forward!

The more you develop, the further away from "perfect" you will find yourself, however at the same time, your life will just become better and better! (Chloe)

Because once you've learnt to let go, you can tackle things as they come, and *that* gives you freedom!

SEE! THIS IS WELL WORTH THINKING ABOUT!

~

Personal notes and comments:

CHAPTER 10

THE LUDICROUS WITHIN THE POSITIVE AND THE NEGATIVE

How, and more importantly, *what* do you think of yourself, your skills, your options, your intellect, your appearance, or your value as a person? What do you think about yourself in relation to your partner, your parents, your colleagues, etc.?

What is *your* most common thought pattern; positive and uplifting or negative and limiting thoughts?

If you belong to the majority, you will probably say that it's the negative and limiting thoughts that are most prevalent!

Just try to think for a moment: *What if somebody spoke to your children in the fashion that you talk to yourself!* What would you want to do or say to them?

Not only would you not allow them, nor accept their opinion, but you will more than likely want to scream at them: *WHO do you think you are? Who invited you to butt in? Go to hell! I'll teach you a lesson!*

No one should talk to your children in that fashion. Not even you! Then why on earth do you allow yourself to think and talk in this fashion about yourself? How then can it be that *this* is acceptable, and that it is "right" and everything else is "wrong"?

How would you react if you were compelled to think and speak nicely about and to yourself?

Can you look at yourself in the mirror (*without* cracking up with laughter) and say to yourself: *Gosh, I'm adorable! Wow, I look absolutely fantastic! I really like myself! I'm the best! I am smart, intelligent and talented...!*

Or is that *so* far from your truths and self perception that it feels almost ludicrous to say and hear these things? (In my experience, men generally are more at ease saying these things to themselves then most women are).

Maybe you can feel both the cramps of laughter or tears, feel your stomach and throat contract, feel how you have to force the air through your constricted throat past your frozen vocal chords; feel how your teeth are clenched and your words have to be prized through your sealed lips: *I really like myself! I'm adorable! I look absolutely fantastic! I'm the best!*

Try it! Try to make yourself aware of the sentences that cause you the most difficulty! What are they about?

Are they about your appearance or your self-esteem? Are they about your abilities or opportunities? Is it just when you have to praise yourself and believe that you *are* the best and that *you* deserve the best?

What happens physically and which thoughts spring to mind?

What do the voices say? The voices you know only too well! The voices that have held you on a short leash for many years, and which with authority, invincible power and conviction only tell you the "truth"!

They tell you that what you are trying to say doesn't ring true, because then the visions of previous experiences and examples flood through your mind's eye, and the voices thunder in your ears, about all the times where you misjudged, failed, were defeated, showed your lack of skills, were ridiculed, and why you of all people don't deserve it!

Who do you think you are? How can you possibly think that you, with the way you are, and look, could ever be desired or worthy of love?

Your eyes see something totally different in the mirror from what you try to tell yourself!

The well known and persistent voices are trying really hard to knock a little "sense" into you so that you can relate to "reality"!

The reality, which relates to the life you're living right now, is what your subconscious is desperately trying to hang on to, because the subconscious doesn't want change! Any change is a direct threat to your whole existence, if you have to ask your subconscious! The most important task our subconscious serves is to keep us safe and give us exactly what we think we need, be it good or bad, positive or negative.

Woe betide anyone who tries to "rock the boat"!

Your inner reality and your self-conception can be based on total fiction, on something that has *nothing* at all to do with the real world, but on something that you have created about yourself, your possibilities and your life! (*See Chapter 5*)

If you try saying something else in front of the mirror, it will sound so ludicrous and far from anything you can relate to!

But, there is really nothing more ludicrous than the fact that it is the negative, the limiting and the self-destructive, which we accept as the truth, that it is this self-created "reality" that we indomitably uphold and defend tooth and nail!

Shouldn't it be the other way around?

Shouldn't we say: *Isn't it actually more ludicrous that I can have these thoughts about myself, when in reality things are very different?*

How is it that such a "reality" evolves into this? Why is it that we, despite the fact that it might keep us stuck in a miserable life, convince ourselves that it is the only truth?

Brian Tracy says in *The Law of Belief*: *Whatever we believe with feeling becomes our reality and if we wish to change our reality we must change our belief about ourselves in relation to reality. If we have self limiting beliefs, they come true for us irrespective of whether or not they are based on fact or fiction!*

What we need to do is change our conscious thoughts about ourselves. We must reassess our expectations of ourselves!

In *The Law of Expectation*, Brian Tracy goes on to say: *Whatever we expect with confidence becomes our own self-fulfilling prophecy. That's why it's absolutely essential that we continually expect the best from ourselves and expect the best of every situation! We find that the most successful men and women make a habit of developing positive self expectancy. They are continually manufacturing their own expectations to keep themselves positive and to keep their self-fulfilling prophecies consistent with what they want to accomplish rather than with what they fear!*

It *is* therefore of utmost importance that we, to achieve the success we desire and to live the life we've dreamed about, constantly have high and positive expectations for ourselves along with having a positive vision and high self-esteem!

About the third law, *The Law of Attraction*, which incidentally happens to be the most known and talked about of the *Laws of The Universe*, especially after the film and book "*The Secret*", Brian Tracy goes on to say: *We inevitably attract into our lives the people and circumstances that harmonize with our dominant thoughts. Therefore if we want to attract different people and different circumstances we have to change our thinking! Our thoughts are like a form of electric magnetic energy that radiates out from us and that attracts back to us those people and circumstances that harmonize with them!*

Our mind or our consciousness is like a garden as James Allen writes in his book *"As a Man Thinketh,"* and in a garden either flowers or weeds will grow!

It is imperative that you understand the importance of this, for whatever you dwell on and stay focused on, whatever you "sow" with your conscious thoughts, will be accepted by your subconscious – totally uncensored – where it will grow and sooner or later will come to manifest itself in your life!

As in the physical world, if you don't consciously plant and tend flowers, water and fertilize them, they will dwindle and die whereas weeds need no tending, nourishment or anything else; in fact they don't even need to be planted! Weeds appear by themselves and if you don't combat them or eradicate them, they will slowly creep in and take over both your garden and in your mind!

In our conscience mind we can only hold one thought at a time, either positive or negative. If we compare the negative thoughts to weeds in the garden, then we need to combat them by *purposely* "planting flowers," thinking positive thoughts.

The art is not just planting them, but to a much higher degree to *cultivate* the positive thoughts and focus so that your life, your "garden" is filled with the most beautiful blooming and colourful flowers.

However ludicrous it may sound and how hard your subconscious fights against your "new" thoughts, your new positive vision of yourself and your forward looking focus, *this* is the only thing, you should be concentrating on changing because if you can change these thoughts, then there are no limits to what you can achieve in your life!

Confront yourself with the utterly ludicrous fact that *you* think talking and thinking positive about yourself is ridiculous! Decide that you will turn the negative and self-destructive thoughts into the "ridiculous", and the positive and constructive thoughts into your "new and true reality." Know for certain that you *can* turn the positive thoughts into a completely natural part of your thought and behavioural patterns, just as the negative thoughts were before!

It takes time to change a habit, and in the beginning you can expect to face very difficult and very stubborn forces! But if you stay the course, hold fast, you will eventually win through!

You will win - YES!

But always bear in mind that it is your dominant thoughts that win through, irrespective of whether they are positive or negative thoughts that you focus on!

So is your "garden", your life, going to be filled with flowers? Or will you really accept your "truths" that are actually nothing but weeds in your mind, as being the right ones, and are you going to allow *them* to dig in and take hold of your life?

THE CHOICE IS YOURS!

~

Personal notes and comments:

CHAPTER 11

"THE RED BELL PEPPERS"

Time and again I find that things I have heard and read many times before *suddenly* sink in and make sense. Every time I read the same book or the same text, listen to the same training either at a seminar or on my MP3 player, I read, see or hear something else, something more, something new. Sometimes it seems as if it were the first time I'd heard or read it, and I am just as amazed every time. It's as if some of the pieces suddenly fall into place and a whole new picture emerges before my eyes!

Until I started working seriously on my personal development, following my mentors' advice, my life was full of thoughts and behavioural patterns that were based on shortcomings, limitations, grievances, deprivation, explanations, and excuses; my life was one as a "victim", governed by outside influences and circumstances!

It was a life where I denied any responsibility for where I stood and what I had, or more accurately what I didn't have, because it was crystal clear to me that nothing was my fault!

Thoughts like the following flitted through my mind: *I'm not good enough. I'm not intelligent. Life is so hard and difficult! There is not enough money! Money doesn't grow on trees! If you need to earn more money you need to work harder and more often! Work before pleasure!* It was: *Ohh... Poor me!*

These thoughts were drilled into me from infancy and I heard them constantly throughout my upbringing. I learnt that I needed to work slavishly and work even harder if I was to earn more. *If* I wanted to allow myself to enjoy life I had to take care of *everything* that needed to be sorted out first!

When you live by the dictum that everything has to be perfect and that you are not allowed to enjoy before you have performed your tasks, there is not much room for a quality lifestyle. But on the rare occasions when I could allow myself a brief moment of freedom, it was with constant bad conscience, guilt and stomach aches. (*See Chapter 9*)

For many years I have listened to and participated in seminars hosted by some of the biggest names in the field of personal development, including Jim Rohn, Bob Proctor, Brian Tracy, Zig Ziglar, Denis Waitley, Vic Johnson, Lisa Jimenez, Gerry Robert and many more, and every time I have been confronted with this very basic principle: *You are and get what you think! You are responsible for your own life, your feelings, any situation you are in and everything you attract into your life! Before things can change, you must change yourself! Before things can get better, you have to become better!*

I thought I understood all this. I could go on quoting many of these very wise people, but at the same time (because of my ingrained thought patterns) I would be provoked by the meaning of these quotes, if I began to think too deeply about them. It was much easier and safer to just go around quoting "the learned ones" to make myself sound clever!

It would take me many years of intense work with my mentors before I completely understood and really absorbed this knowledge! My life has not been the same ever since, and it continues to evolve and expand in its diversity of opportunities and wealth!

James Allen, who among other things wrote "*As a Man Thinketh*" over a hundred years ago, has for decades inspired some of the greatest thinkers and inspirators with his interpretation of the power of thought: *That you are and get what you think!*

He also wrote: *You are today where your thoughts have brought you – you will be tomorrow where your thoughts take you!* This is one of the toughest things to stomach!

When you live the life of a "victim" as I did, you don't need to accept responsibility for anything, especially not your own life or the situations you find yourself in! But the day when you really understand and finally *accept* responsibility for where you are and for what you have, from that day on you are finally finished complaining and placing blame on others or other things!

On the one side it is very frightening that you can no longer hide behind others and accuse and blame others for the "mess" you're in. Then, on the other side, it is the most liberating revelation and decision you can make, because just by understanding and accepting that *everything* is created by your *own* thoughts and actions, this will allow you the freedom and opportunity to change your situation and create the life you really want!

You can be the one who finally break the stereotypical thoughts and behavioural patterns, which for generations might have kept you and your family trapped in a life that no one basically wants or thrives in, but one which you've merely accepted as your destiny and place in life!

Why then are there actually so few, who choose this path? So few who really take it upon themselves and create the most fulfilling life that they could ever want, a life filled with contentment, love and abundance on all levels!

It is one thing to understand and accept. It is something completely different to make the decision to change your thoughts and thereby your life, but there is one other very deciding factor for this to succeed, and that is perseverance!

To *keep going until...*!

When we try to alter something in our lives, our subconscious and our thought patterns will battle each other so that things can continue in the same familiar way as they were before! (*See Chapter10*)

Our subconscious will always see anything new as a potential enemy and a danger that threatens our existence, and rightly so, because if we allow the new thoughts to enter, we are then compelled to discard the old ones! Until the old thoughts are totally discarded, the new thoughts can't be absorbed! Both the previous thoughts and situations will continue to rear their ugly heads until we have learnt the lessons that have to be learnt for each given situation.

As a progressive and evolving being, man is where he is that he may learn that he may grow; and as he learns the spiritual lesson which any circumstance contains for him, it passes away and gives place to other circumstances. (James Allen)

It is from the greatest challenges and adverse circumstances that you will grow and learn the most! Today I am deeply grateful for the challenges and opposition I have encountered, for it is these that have taught me the most, made me stronger and turned me into who I am today!

If you have tried to alter some of your old habits and thought patterns, for example, your own perception of yourself or your self-awareness, then you can relate to what I'm talking about!

You will recognize the violent struggle, often with physical reactions within your body, and your mind will battle through to thwart and defeat the new!

If we don't grab the bull by the horns and immediately overthrow the old thought patterns and actions – our paradigms – which Bob Proctor often refers to, they will persevere and we will have to capitulate and convince ourselves that *it just wasn't for us!*

We may well have many good intentions, goals and dreams, but as long as our subconscious and mindset remain unchanged, there will not be any form of change or development in our lives! It is precisely this part that often causes confusion and frustration for most people who *really want to* change their lives!

James Allen further writes: *A person is the causer (though nearly always unconsciously) of his circumstances, and that, whilst aiming at the good end, he is continually frustrating its accomplishment by encouraging thoughts and desires which cannot possibly harmonize with that end!*

If we live with a "poverty mentality" and don't change it, we will always have and attract more of what we think about, namely tough times, errors, shortages, limitations and a lack of money!

So, regardless of how much we may desire to be wealthy or wish to change our lives, *nothing* will change until we alter our fundamental beliefs and our thoughts that we have about ourselves and our possibilities and *keep* them changed!

Gerry Robert, author of *"A Millionaire Mindset"*, explains very succinctly his own experiences with this situation:

He grew up in difficult times, in poverty and with an alcoholic father, so Gerry had already learnt from early childhood and all through his adolescence that life *was* tough! There was never enough money; everything was so expensive, etc.

He managed later in life to break out of these thoughts and lifestyle patterns, just by taking responsibility for his own life and *purposely* creating the life he had always dreamed of!

When Gerry's accountant one day came and told him that in the previous month Gerry had earned over US$200,000, it was both pleasing and almost completely incomprehensible to him! Gerry explained that he decided to take the rest of the day off and drive home and celebrate the great news with his wife. He rang her and said he was coming home early and had something important to tell her. She, unaware of what the news entailed, replied: *Fine, will you please buy some groceries on your way home?*

Gerry stopped to shop as he was asked to, and as he was placing items in his basket, red bell peppers too among other things, something which ever since childhood had been one of his favourite foods, he heard a well-remembered voice (his mother's) say: *No Gerry, they are too expensive, put them back!*

On his way to the checkout it struck him: *There* he was, a man in his forties, who had just earned over US$200,000 in the last month and he actually replaced the red peppers "just" because the familiar voice said they were too expensive!

Wow! Just think about that!

How many "red peppers" have *you* put back because that was how it once was? Based on a restrictive mindset, one which you have accepted because that's what you grew up hearing!

It is important to understand that while Gerry, in his narrative, is in his forties and *has* already experienced great success in many areas of his life, he, *like most others* (yourself included), still has many voices and rigid thought patterns from his upbringing.

In every situation or task that we have to complete, we have a "self-conception", a vision or perception of ourselves, i.e., what we think or believe we can or can't do!

It is therefore of the utmost importance that you understand that you have to continue your personal growth and learning process throughout your life! It is not something that ends, you just become better and better at tackling the challenges as they arrive, and you will more quickly be able to "rebound" and move forward!

There will be no development or growth in your life without challenges. So, instead of fighting them and wishing them to be gone, we should "leap into the fray" and find the insight and wisdom needed to confront the challenges. Only by taking this approach will these challenges be resolved, and you will have more clarity, strength, wisdom and insight, to tackle the next challenge. It is these that give life colour and excitement!

This is also why there is no "perfect"! So even if you succeed in fulfilling your wildest dreams, for example, becoming a multi-millionaire or a world famous actor, model, author or sports personality, you will, just like Gerry, myself, and many others, have rigid and restrictive thoughts about yourself in different areas of your life.

We are all only human and it is basically this that makes us so unique and amazing!

Set yourself a target to get to know yourself better. Search deep down and pay attention to the voices and thoughts you have, because *you* can change them – *you* can alter and create *your* life instead of continuing with the life you lead, which you have unwittingly and unconsciously made yours!

This, however, requires that you first find out *what* it is you really want, *then* which restricting thoughts and actions you have accepted and made your "truths" about yourself and your opportunities here in life!

You will need to be aware of where you currently stand, before you can move forward to your new goals! It's not enough just to have a goal or a dream. If you don't know where you stand now, or which thoughts control your mind and thereby your life, it will be like just plotting your *destination* into your GPS.

How can it give you instructions about your journey or direction if it doesn't know where you're starting from or where you are now?

If you don't know what rigid thoughts and actions you have made your own and according to which truths you live your life by, then you will be unable to confront them and change them!

It might well be a thought, a vision of yourself and your own abilities that you have absorbed as your own truth. You must be able to relate critically to it, and realize that the sole purpose of it is to restrict you as to why you deserve to have success. Then this vision or self-perception will always serve as a hindrance in your life and you will, on a subconscious level, always contest or sabotage the success you previously have fought so hard to achieve!

You see it time and time again. Some people manage to get involved in something that looks promising and which, if successful, could change their life and lifestyle forever, but because an opulent life, a life as a successful person, is so far from their self-perception and habitual thoughts, they will manage to create (obviously unintentionally) situations that hinder and ruin things, just when they are in the process of finally succeeding!
The new successful life is simply too distant from the vision they have of themselves and the life they think they deserve or are destined to live!

One hand places the "red peppers" in the basket, while the

other just as quickly empties it and replaces them on the shelf, while the well known voices continue trying to knock some "sense" into your head!

It requires determination and strength to change your life for the better!

It takes courage to face the fact that the life you live – the situations and circumstances you have in your life right now – is something you have created by the thoughts you have about yourself!

We are all at the place in our lives where we deserve to be! We are where our vision of ourselves allows us to be!

Most have a vision of themselves that is not consistent with their wishes!

There are many people who desire a life of economic stability, contentment and success, but from where they currently stand, they can't see themselves achieving it! Many feel they are worth more than what their employer pays them in wages, and they also believe that they should have greater responsibility at work. The problem is that very few can, for a longer period of time, continue in a manner that is not consistent with their vision of themselves.

Very few think about how they see themselves or how they talk to themselves: *I can't, and I will never amount to anything. This is how we have always done things in our family, etc*. Here then, the question arises: Is it right for them to think like this about themselves and their lives? (*See Chapter 10*)

Where in their lives, are those who taught you your thought patterns? Do they have the life and success that you want? If not, why copy them? Why listen to people who don't live the life you desire? Maybe it's about time to change the way you talk and think about yourself. The vast majority of people who have achieved success in this world say unanimously that the way they talk and think about themselves has been one of the most crucial elements for their success in life!

Nevertheless, you hear countless people saying things like: *I don't believe that will work! You can't get a better life with more contentment just by talking differently to yourself!*

But honestly, how can you tell if you've never done it or tried it yourself? If you've never been aware of your thoughts and what you say to and about yourself each day?

Consistently sticking to positive thoughts about yourself does make a huge difference!

Our subconscious is like a computer, which accepts everything we put into it with our conscious thoughts!

It takes courage to stand up, persevere and to go against the flow! When you change yourself, you will invariably lose some from your circle of friends and others may drop you.

Therefore, knowledge of *what* it is that you want, and *where* you want to go, and just as importantly, *where* you "stand" right now, is so essential for you to progress and succeed!

You need to maintain focus and be clear! You must know your *"why(s)"*!

If you don't have enough reasons with respect to why you should continue when things seem bleak, and the struggle is hardest felt, then like the majority you will just choose to quit and stagnate in the life you have now!

You need to constantly remind yourself, especially when things feel most difficult, that *Success lies on the other side of quitting!* (*See Chapter 8*)

Try to remember these three things that Les Brown recommends next time you're on the verge of quitting:

1) Have faith!

2) Remind yourself: No matter how hard it is or how hard it gets, I'm going to make it!

3) Have patience and engage in consistent action!

Without *faith* the next two points have no meaning, and even if you practice the second point as your daily mantra, you'll get nowhere without points one and three!

Lack of patience, perseverance and *daily* action are often where most go wrong!

Many people purchase a book or a programme and maybe they even attend a couple of seminars, but when the seminar is over, the book has been read and the programme has been listened to, then they are put away or forgotten. Then it's back to everyday life and you will hear the same people say: *I've tried, I've done it, but it didn't help! It didn't work!*

No one says it quite like Zig Ziglar, simply and directly:

People often say that motivation doesn't last!
Well, neither does bathing! That's why we recommend it daily!

Equally clear is this message, which for many is an almost painfully embarrassing truth: *To know but not to do, is not to know!*

Remember: Knowledge without action leads nowhere!

So make sure *you* take control over your own life! Ensure you plot your starting point and destination, your ultimate goal, into your "GPS" and decide that you're going to go the whole way! Be sure to nip it in the bud, and give the "hand" that tries to get you to put your "red pepper" back on the shelf a very sharp rap on the knuckles!

You should only fill your life's "basket" with everything *your* heart desires!

In *this* way you can go from the life you have now, to the new life created by *yourself, on your own terms and according to your own dreams!*

~

Anyone can give up; it's the easiest thing in the world to do! But to hold it together when everyone else would understand if you fell apart: that's true strength!

Ambrose Redmoon

~

Personal notes and comments:

CHAPTER 12

WHAT'S ACTUALLY THE WORST THAT CAN HAPPEN?

You've probably heard others ask this question and may even have asked yourself the same thing: *What's actually the worst that can happen?*

You can be so paralysed and stuck by "panic" in a given situation that you completely forget to take a step back, just breathe deeply and then repeat that question to yourself: *What's actually the worst that can happen?*
Most often it is thoughts, anxiety and panic that overtake us and assume unprecedented and completely unrealistic proportions!

Basically there are no reasons why we worry ourselves – either we can solve the problem, or we can't!

"The Serenity Prayer" (written by theologian Reinhold Niebuhr in the late 1930s / early 1940s) reads: *God grant me the serenity to accept the things I cannot change, courage to change the things I can and the wisdom to know the difference!*

James Allen writes: *Thoughts of doubt and fear can never accomplish anything! They always lead to failure!*

Bob Proctor remarks: *The fear of failure is the greatest single obstacle to success in adult life. Fear of failure is what holds more people back from exploring their potential than any other factor in human personality!*

It has been said that we are born with only three forms of anxiety: the fear of falling, the fear of loud noises and then the last, as many of the experts also deem to be congenital, namely the fear of being abandoned or rejected!

All other forms of anxiety are learned through life, but most of them have been founded in early childhood. The most prevalent of them, which often accompanies people throughout their lives, are the fear of defeat, the fear of "losing face" and the fear of success! These are for most people, definitely some of the biggest hurdles against achieving their desire and going after their own dreams!

Generally you can say that anxiety, in all its forms, is the greatest enemy in life, because it prevents us from doing many of the things we really want to do and that could make our lives even more amazing, contented and richer!

Try for a moment to pause – put this book down – and reflect back over your own life!

How many times have you stopped yourself and have avoided doing what *you* really wanted to do, because fear has dominated your thoughts? I mean the fear of what others might think, or of whether you were really good or clever enough, or the fear of being rejected or left out if you did something other than what you *assumed* the others would do! If you reflect back on your life with a critical eye, you will wonder if it *is your* life you're living.

Can you honestly say that everything you do is done based entirely on what suits your own needs, desires, dreams and values?

No, because if you did you wouldn't be in your current situation!

One thing is *anxiety*, which many allow themselves to be

steered by; another is its precursor – *doubt!*

Doubt is not something we are born with. The habit of doubting (e.g. If we can handle a specific task, whether we are good enough, whether we deserve it...etc.), grows throughout life, but it is most often founded in our early childhood and for some, doubts end up being very strong and very destructive to the individual's ability to live a full and complete life!

If we allow doubt to take over and overwhelm us completely, it will flourish from the first little shadow to an anxiety so enormous that it may even trigger a physical reaction!

Look at this wise saying: *A doubting mind will be so unstable, so easy to unbalance, like a boat on troubled waters and every decision will be uncertain, when you first go one way and then another!*

If most of our anxiety and *all* our doubts are conceived during our upbringing, then we should be able to overcome them and learn to master them by learning to control our thoughts!

Mark Twain once said: *True courage is not about the absence of fear, it is the mastery of fear!*

People who live their lives according to their own dreams and values experience just as much anxiety as those who live a miserable, discontented and unsatisfying life – the former have just learned to master their fears instead of being ruled by them!

In this context Ambrose Redmoon, adds: *Courage is not the absence of fear, but rather the judgment that something else is more important than fear.*

Every single person has experienced or is experiencing anxiety! Those who manage to overcome and manage their anxiety are those who have shifted their focus from fear over to what is most important to them!

One example I think we all can relate to regarding anxiety and fear is in a situation where your little child runs out into the road! In this situation you will easily overcome your own fear of whether or not you can do it, OR what others may think, or whether something might happen to you. Your doubts about whether or not you should act immediately disappear! There is suddenly nothing more important than saving your child!

Absolutely!

But why, then, do we not accord the same high priority to how we live the life we really desire and dream about? Why even have any doubts or fears about whether you're doing the right thing, whether it is good enough, or what others might think?

What does it mean for you to live the life you dream about, and what will it mean for your well-being, your confidence and your pride, and what surplus energy will it give you that you can use on all the good things in this life, so as to help others to live their life to the fullest?

YES! *What's actually the worst that can happen*

Try to focus on what is "behind" – on the other side of your anxiety!

Focus on what really is important to you in your life!

What kind of life do you want to live, now that you have overcome your anxiety and taken control of your life?

Now we know it all begins with doubt. When we give in to a doubt it is allowed to grow and develop into an anxiety. So we must stamp it out and defeat it *before* it is allowed to develop into such an intense anxiety that it completely paralyses us.

As Bob Proctor further states: *It begins precisely with doubt – the doubt is allowed to evolve so that it creates the feeling of anxiety, which then manifests itself physically as anxiety and restlessness. Anxiety robs us of our power, our energy and our purpose!*

Major or severe anxiety may even undermine our health and make us sick and all this is triggered by merely a small feeling of doubt, which was not stopped in time!

It appears that the two (anxiety and doubt) are almost inseparable! The whole thing is a self-perpetuating and downward spiral!
You can almost wonder which actually came first just as in the case of the chicken and the egg.

Too many look at their lives here and now and highlight the many reasons why they obviously are experiencing both doubt and anxiety! It's these external causes, the way things are, that keep them stuck in their miserable or maybe relatively "boring" lives.

It becomes the external causes, their "here and now" situation gets the blame, and then the person becomes or makes of themselves a "poor victim"!

YES, things are connected! It *is* a chain reaction! But it is *you* who are in charge, it is you, who can regain control and take over the running of *your* life! Only you and you alone can turn things around, weather the storm and the "here and now" problems, and steer towards life's sun-drenched shores of your choice!

It all starts with taking control of your thoughts!

You must control your conscious thoughts, stamp out doubts as soon as they appear and maintain your focus on what is really important to you and your life!

Stop and take an outside look at the situation so that you can get a better perspective on what is happening and what you are in the midst of, and ask yourself, preferably aloud: *What's actually the worst thing that can happen? What is actually real here? What is reality, the true facts, and what is my self-created reality?*

Are the thoughts I have about myself, my abilities, my doubts, and my anxieties substantiated and if so, in relation to what?

Just think that such a little element of doubt can cause so much devastation!

Just think that the power of thought is *so* strong!

But what actually is even more sobering and amazing is that you can learn to manage it by consciously changing and controlling your thoughts! You must therefore firstly change your mindset and your thoughts when the doubt arises, and then you must *keep it changed!*

It's actually the first of three things you can do to overcome the doubt *before* it evolves into an even more devastating anxiety! The fact is that what you are thinking consciously will eventually be heard and accepted as the truth by your subconscious, and it will then become your new "belief" and everything will work towards precisely this happening!

You receive what you think, and what you focus on, good as well as bad! Always remember this!

So if your focus is only on shortcomings, errors, and failures, then those are what you will attract more of into your life, but if you are able to change this negative and limited thinking into conscious, positive "thoughts of abundance", then eventually it will be this abundance that you will get more of in your life!

If you, for example, always doubt or fret over not having

enough money to last the whole month, then instead, alter your thoughts to the positive, so that when doubts rear their ugly heads counteract them by confirmation, by saying something like, *I always have more than enough of everything I need!*

Emmet Fox wrote: *If you will change your mind concerning anything and absolutely keep it changed, that thing must and will change too. It is the keeping up of the change in thought that is difficult. It calls for vigilance and determination!*

The second thing you can and must do is: *Do the thing you fear and fear will disappear.* We've probably all heard this said before, maybe in other forms, but basically it's about doing what you fear (or are anxious about), because once it's done, once the boundary *is* crossed, then it will never be the same again. The next time you face the same challenge, the "fear of success" will be much less because you've already done it before and survived!

When you want to overcome your anxiety, go beyond your boundaries and expand your comfort zone. In this respect it is worth remembering that you can choose a totally different, perhaps even more challenging, task to try and accomplish. Once you have overcome what you originally faced (as something most fearsome), it suddenly seems like a minor challenge!

The fact that you in other areas of your life seek challenges and exceed boundaries, gives you the strength, and more than that, it gives you "evidence" that you *can* tackle even more difficult and bigger challenges!
Each time you exceed your boundaries, you actually expand your comfort zone, become stronger, increase your confidence and grow as a person!

Another of Reinhold Niebuhr's famous quotes refers to just that: *If we survive danger it steels our courage more than anything else!*

So be thankful for all the challenges you have or will experience in your life, for they are the ones that give you the strength and the wisdom to progress in your life!

If you choose to live a life without challenges, because you currently think that it is the "nicest" and that everything is easy and problem free, you must also be aware that in this safe and secure life there aren't any special opportunities for development and growth!

The vast majority prefer the aforementioned security rather than development, change and growth. But if you are among those who *want* more out of life and who know there is more to life than what you have right now, realise that it is only through constant and conscious work on yourself, your thoughts, your behavioural patterns and the challenges you encounter, that you will be able to develop and grow!

The third and probably the most important tool to overcome your doubts and anxiety is *belief!* Anxiety and belief are direct opposites in your life, for your options and your future, and they can't both be present at the same time!

Belief is, and always will be, the strongest and will overcome anxiety and fear every time!

First, you must know what *you* want! When you keep focus on what matters most in your life, when you decide that you will live *your* life and not a life ruled by doubt and anxiety, based on what you had earlier accepted as "the truth" about yourself and your capabilities, then you will be given the opportunity to live the most amazing and full life you can dream of!

But if you let doubt and anxiety rule and you do not know what you want, then you will live a life left to chance and without any kind of self-monitoring! If you live a life of compromise and for others' wishes and dreams, or how you *think* others will want you to live your life, can you really say that you are living?

I heard an 'amusing' anecdote about an insurance company, which refused to pay out a policy on a now deceased husband's life insurance to the bereaved, because they claimed that he never really lived!

Wow! Imagine this becoming a reality one day!

How many or *how few* would then really be sure that they could assess their time on earth, as a life that was lived to the full?

Isn't it true that we all wish that the dash between the two dates on our tombstones stood for more than just a dash? Should it not symbolize the most amazing life we have lived and all the incredible experiences we have had?

Should it not stand for and represent: *A RICHER LIFE – LIVED TO THE FULL?*

Doesn't everything else then seem totally irrelevant?

The more you begin to live – the more of life you let in – the easier it becomes to prioritize and when doubts arise, ask yourself: *whose life do I want to live?*

Remember...

IF YOU WANT TO LIVE LARGE, SEEK THE LARGEST CHALLENGES!

~

Personal notes and comments:

CHAPTER 13

THE GENDER POWER STRUGGLE –
AND WHERE DOES SEX APPEAR IN THE EQUATION?

One of the biggest stumbling blocks I have experienced has been my view of myself regarding to what I was worth as a person, and consequently, what I felt I deserved, or rather did not deserve to enjoy, do or have!
But how did enjoyment and whether I deserved to feel good become so forbidden in my mind?

I had somehow programmed into my subconscious that I could not and did not deserve to feel good, and that I did not deserve to enjoy, at least not until *after* things had been sorted out, and certainly not enjoy something like sex for sex is firstly not something "nice girls" have or enjoy, and *if* it does happen, it's definitely not something to explore and experiment with! It was not advisable to indulge in hot and frantic sex, and in ecstasy forgetting all about time and place!

Only just plain ordinary sex, almost "obligatory sex", was allowed in my mind, almost just so that my partner could get his release, and *then* I could get on with the much *more important* tasks that waited, because really there was no time for such nonsense!

How many women live this way where sex is something that must be dealt with, wondering how it is ever allowed a space in the relationship at all!

Because we women so often feel that first things must be in

place or in order *before* we can let go, let our hair down and then think it's okay to enjoy!

How many women do not use sex – or rather the lack thereof – as a weapon of power in the home and in their relationship? *It is out of the question! Who is he to think that he can just come here and want sex, when the whole house is in an uproar, food has to be prepared, the children have to be taken care of, etc.!*

So if the man (in the woman's opinion) does not help or do enough at home, then she punishes him; and what is the best way a woman can control a man? She denies him sex!

We women see it as our right and our "trump card" and we can go about rejoicing in our strength, and the fact that we women apparently find it easier to walk around for a longer period of time without sex; it can take days, weeks, months that way and the longer it goes on like this, the harder it becomes to break the ice and to get it going again because isn't there always something that *just* needs to be put right or to be changed?

Most women basically desire to be ravished by a MAN, to see and feel his strength. We want to let go, feel helpless in his powerful arms, and secretly wish that it is a "primordial man" with the basic instincts taking over! But... *ONLY* when it suits us!

Woe betide the man who tries to "take us" when there is a pile of washing-up to be done and dirty laundry is scattered all over the floor!

Yes, it's almost farcical: *Ah come and ravish me my big, strong man*, our body almost screams! Then the brain kicks in and what comes out of our mouth is: *What on earth are you thinking? Now's not the time! Can't you see this and that needs to be sorted out first!*

It is not exactly conducive to the mood or his attempts at being manly!

I also believe that when mixed together with many women's feelings of guilt and bad conscience in general, it can actually enhance the reaction and rejection!

What is it about us women and sex? Where have we learned this pattern of using sex (denial of sex) as a weapon of power? Most of our learned perceptions, our thinking and behavioural patterns, are founded in early childhood and adolescence!

How was it in our home when we were growing up? What did we see at home? How was the relationship between our parents? Did we observe love and tenderness, see a relaxed and natural attitude to each other and a relationship where there was love and warm feelings for each other? Was sex a relaxed and natural part of a healthy relationship/marriage? Of course I'm *not* referring to sex openly indulged in the children's presence but if touching, caressing, joy, feelings and love for each other was openly displayed and shared!

Or did we see (as children pick up much more than just what is said with words) a relationship where emotions were never displayed, but instead there was a constant power struggle raging between our parents?

We grew up in an era where women had to be just as strong as men and where men should be just as soft and sensitive as women.

We have created the soft man, the one who is "ever so understanding" and does just as much housework as the woman. He should be able to look after children, cook, tidy up, clean, do the washing and iron clothes!

On top of all that, he must also be our hero, big and strong, who comes to conquer and ravish us – but of course *ONLY* when it suits us!

In other words, he must go out and conquer and impress the entire world, but be home by 4 p.m.!

What is it that these power struggles between the sexes have achieved? Can we really talk about an equalization of the sexes? We must at all costs be the same, but it is especially the woman who must be strong and be able to do everything herself, and the man who must be like a woman!

For *this* is the right way, and now it's no more of being the oppressed sex! It's almost as if we are thinking: *Now let him taste some of his own medicine* and then he comes to "pay" for all the years of oppression of women!

Many have grown up in broken families and certainly managed to experience parental problems and quarrels before their parents eventually divorced. Many experienced a relationship where the woman became stronger and stronger and the man weaker and weaker and where he was eventually turned into a puppet and sissy!

It was what many of us saw, learned and, therefore, have carried with us into our own adult lives!

This power struggle has drained and destroyed many relationships and in many situations may well have killed any sexual desire left!

When the respect disappears, there's nothing left to build a relationship on. For how can one have respect for a sissy of a husband who can't take a decision alone and allows himself to be domineered by a woman who manages the home with an iron fist and "turns off the hot water" (denies him sex) when things aren't going to her liking or when she thinks that he isn't helping enough?

We women have "created" men in the way that we wanted them, but then when they have become like us – there's not much fun in it anymore! It may be hard for us to turn on or have sex with such a soft and "understanding" man. A man that the woman now feels more like a mother to! A man without virility and strength, without an independent opinion, a man who lets himself be cow towed and bends like the grass in the wind!

But do we women become inferior, weaker as a gender, if we let the man be a man? If we in our relationship allow him to be and to perform as a man – and during sex let him show his masculine power and ravish us – isn't it what many of us actually yearn for deep down?

Like most others, I love sex and when I have it and enjoy it nowadays – when I let go and give in to the pleasure – then I can't understand or see any meaning in my previous reaction and my attempt to punish the man by refusing to have sex, because, as I can see it now, I basically punished myself, didn't I?

Is there anything better than to lie there close with your beloved after a good session of sex? Is there anything that can get you to relax and forget the daily rigors as a good sex session and some great orgasms? No, there isn't!

Doesn't a good sex session, or even just a "quickie", give both pleasure and the feeling of extreme closeness? Isn't sex just even more helpful in making everyday work a bit more fun and manageable?

Why then did I think to punish my husband by denying him sex?

It was the ingrained thoughts and behavioural patterns in my family that were the ones I observed and accepted while I was growing up, and of course the attitude and the perception that "nice girls" do not have sex. It is only "cheap" girls who have and enjoy sex which, as with all the other pleasures in life, could only be allowed, once you had earned it!

It was a challenge at the beginning of my current relationship, sometimes an enormous challenge, that now I had met a real man, a man who is adamant that he is a man and that there are things he is good at and things that I, as a woman, am good at and that this is not something that should be standardized or changed, but that differences in fact can be a strength!

It went so much against everything that I had grown up with and had learned. It was contrary to what I and so many other women had seen and learned about the man obviously having to help with everything at home.

That *everything* should be divided equally, rather than from what each individual had as strengths and resources to offer to the relationship!

In return, I experienced over time that my femininity evolved and that I grew as a woman and that I am today respected more than ever for the person I am!

I've learned to love and appreciate the differences and can see how much more dynamism there can be in a relationship where the man is a man and the woman is a woman! I now see what it means for the relationship when you respect each other for who you are and what each can do, rather than fighting the differences!

I feel I have become even more of a woman now that I have found a MAN and the more I let him be a man and constantly confirm this to him, the more like a woman I am allowed to be and feel. In other words, a win/win situation for both parties!

When the power struggle ceases and differences are valued and appreciated, then respect and feelings grow and that in turn gives you both more energy and contentment!

When your sex life becomes a priority and is pleasurable and harmonious, then the relationship gets even better and when the relationship works, everyday runs better and when life functions well, everyone thrives, both children and adults!

The fact that it is diversity that gives strength to the relationship, and which should be encouraged rather than fought over, has for too long been a taboo subject! Fortunately, I feel this trend in society is changing!

But there are certainly many women still who will continue to stick with what they've learned, namely that the man should be like us women, and that we should all be equal and on the same footing.

These women claim and insist that they want a man who is, and who does, the same as them, and they use "no sex" as a lever to get what they want, and to punish the man with! But these same women complain that they have not got a real man someone who can just take over and make a decision, one that dares to put their foot down if necessary and who dares show his strength and masculinity in the home and in bed!

This mixture of the gender power struggle and your upbringing (which said there are things that have to be "completed" before you can enjoy), and for some women the ideas that "nice girls" *do not or should not enjoy sex*, is probably not the best cocktail, nor particularly conducive to a functioning relationship, and especially not for a favourable and amorous sex life!

When it is mixed with the guilt, shame, and bad conscience that so many are burdened with, it is clear that it all becomes even more difficult to digest and is doomed to become total chaos in all areas!
The confusion becomes complete when the brain and the subconscious mind say one thing, and the body at the same

time craves to feel and experience this great pleasure that sex is!

When we're talking about sex, how are we to enjoy something that is taught or perceived as being so wrong and maybe even banned?

When the power struggle continues, and you may even have this fixed idea that sex and pleasure only can be allowed after the work is completed, how will you ever have a relaxed attitude towards yourself, your partner, or sex?

Could it be that since childhood the enjoyment and prioritizing of each other, and of sex, has been seen as something wrong, taboo, and perhaps even embarrassing and shameful, that so many find it difficult to admit that they enjoy and appreciate the differences and the personal values?

We are more concerned about what others might think and say, if they knew that we were "just" enjoying, enjoying letting go and just being ourselves!

But what others think or say is and should be completely irrelevant when you plan and live your life!

You'll have to let go of old thoughts and behavioural patterns, in order to allow enjoyment and pleasure into your life.

What is basically most important in your life and your relationship? Is it so important that the laundry is sorted *right now*? Does it mean more than togetherness and enjoyment with your partner or your children?

Maybe it's about time that you looked deeper into the priorities of your life! Are they yours? Are they what are best for *your* particular relationships and *your* life? Are they something that strengthens and boosts your relationship and marriage? Or is it a power struggle based on past values, which today we see the

result of, a power struggle in which all parties become losers –
men, women, and especially the children!

For what do the children see and learn whilst they are growing
up?
Is it worth holding on to the "old values"?

Isn't a healthy and equal footed relationship one where you
respect each other for who you are, and what you do?

How about just loving and being curious about exploring the
differences, rather than fighting them and each other?

Choose to be open and fascinated rather than leaving yourself
frustrated and fighting against everything that is good and
unique in yourself, and in your partner!

ENJOY! – LOVE! - LIVE!

Personal notes and comments:

CHAPTER 14

WHAT'S IT LIKE "TO ENJOY"?

What does it mean *to enjoy* and how is it *to enjoy?* Should we have to obtain permission to enjoy? Is it something you can do automatically or something you have to learn to do?

What can you enjoy? Are there any limits? If the answer is YES, then who sets these limits or rules? Do you or do others?

Are there things that need to be in order before you can enjoy? Are there things that need to be sorted out first?

Can you just go around enjoying the whole day? Is there a correct way to enjoy?

When do you know if you're enjoying things enough or correctly?

Is it either: *I enjoy* or *I don't enjoy?*

Is it okay to enjoy something a little bit and still claim to enjoy, or must there be "maximum enjoyment" before it actually counts/applies?

Can you, for example, enjoy your life when everything around you is chaotic – if you are up to your eyes in debt, out of work, ill, handicapped, etc.?

These were some of the questions which sprang to my mind when I decided to write about the topic, *to enjoy.*

How is it that you see people with severe disabilities (either from birth or incurred after an accident or in war) who are still happy and enjoy life and radiate lots of life quality, and who often are a great inspiration for many others?

It *moves* you when you see or hear a person with noticeably larger challenges than you have explain with radiant eyes how amazing life is, and how glad and grateful he/she is to be alive!

It is very difficult not to think: *Oops, how can I sit here and complain to myself that life is tough and unfair, when he/she sits there and is so grateful for life? If THEY can, with all their challenges, then so should I!*

It can often be with some bad conscience that you think back on what you have just sat and cried over and complained about! Sometimes it is actually good to be reminded of just how privileged we actually are, and especially how important it is to *enjoy* the amazing life that we have, *while* we have it! We can become so preoccupied with our "nit picking" that we miss out on enjoying life while we have the chance!

Why shouldn't you enjoy your life, *every single day,* even if this particular time in your life is difficult? What do you think, honestly, helps most right now and in the near future? To sit down and weep, complain and blame, or to choose to have a good day, be content with what you have and enjoy your life as a whole?

One thing is certain: you can't change your situation by lamenting! All this does is keep you convinced that everything is tough and unfair and that there is nothing you can do about it!

Life goes on with or without you and no matter how many minutes, hours or days you spend being discontented, blaming and complaining about your "here and now" situation, this time will *not* come back!

How about the words: *Live life as if each day is your last!* Life *is* short and (luckily) we never know precisely when this life that we know will end! So isn't it better to choose to get the *best* out of *each* day of our lives while we can?

How many people have you heard say: *when I retire, THEN I'll enjoy life?* What is even sadder is, how many of those, just when they are about to enjoy life, suddenly get seriously ill or even worse, die before their time? Just when they are finally able to enjoy *all* the things they had planned to do, now they had finally retired!

By denying enjoyment and thinking for example that something has to wait until we retire, we actually deny the whole essence of life!

ISN'T the meaning of life that we should get the best out of it while we have the chance?

Learn to enjoy and be grateful for what you have! Learn to enjoy and love *despite...* because if we don't choose otherwise, there will always be something or other that *just* needs to be sorted, completed, etc.!

Forget all about "when" and" if"!

It is NOW that you need to live, NOW that you should enjoy, NOW that you should love, NOW that you should be grateful, and NOW that you should be contented and giving!

Maybe, the "being able to enjoy" needs a little help on the way? Maybe you have completely forgotten what and how to enjoy? We are in such a rush these days that we completely forget to pause and simply enjoy, maybe to just enjoy the moment! Take a deep breath and fill your lungs. Look around you and marvel at life's amazing diversity of people, things and nature!

Do you have children? If you have, just think when was the last time that you stopped what you were doing and just sat and watched them? Enjoyed them playing, laughing, crying, sleeping; saw them *living*, being happy and just enjoying (children have this spontaneous and uncomplicated outlook on life right up until we "strip" it from them – because now they need to be grown-up and act like grown-ups, learn to take things seriously and learn that life isn't a game!).

But *why* must things always be so serious? When was the last time you just took a pause to embrace, enjoy and *feel* your husband, wife, partner, children, mother, father, your best friend, your dog, etc.?

A concept, I think, that everyone knows and many have resorted to in order to soothe the worst of their bad conscience about not spending a lot of time with their children, now that we are all so busy, is the concept of *quality time!*

There's nothing like a bad conscience that can make a relationship whittle away (both when it comes to your partner and children), and which can affect the majority of people in their way of "upbringing" – or whatever you call that, which happens in most homes today – where the children are allowed to dictate, and maybe even manipulate, because one or both parents have a bad conscience about how little time they spend with their children!

With quality time, it doesn't mean the amount of hours we spend together, but more that we ensure that the 5-10-15 minutes we spend together are concentrated and a shared closeness! As if 15 minutes of quality time with your child(ren) can encompass the attention, closeness, intimacy and affection a child *has* the need of!

Think about this:

If you ask a child to write the word LOVE, they will always spell it: T-I-M-E!

Look at this extract from an article by Mogens Hansen, former Professor at the Danish University of Education, Allerød:

Small children sense, perceive and experience much slower compared to adults. When you process and experience slower you have need for more time. Where does the term quality time actually come from? It comes from adults who are too busy with their own time and will only devote a small portion of their time to their children. The term is used to cover up a mixture of reluctance to be with their children and a verbal cover-up for the experiences of guilt over the failure to do so.

For small children time's quality isn't 14 minutes closeness but a long, long time spent together with an adult!

For the adult it is the close involvement with the child, to empathize with the child's play and contact in relationship to the adult. So the adult ends up in a practical and mental acquiescence with the child!

Older children can definitely use quality time together with an adult. Close contact of thoughts, feelings and play. When are children "older" or big enough? This is when the child and adult are on an equal footing when being together. You can't set a specific age!

Quality time is a cover-up phrase where many attempt to reflect on a child's life from a theoretical management angle!

Many adults, including parents, educators (primary school teachers) and teachers generally speak too fast when they talk to children. Children listen slowly and actually can't absorb what is being said to them when adults speak rapidly. It is often perceived that children are ignoring and are resisting the adult's requests. This often results in the adult raising their voice and speaking even more rapidly.

So: Adults talk too fast, while the children listen slowly!

One of the letters, which resulted from the above article, was written by "Vibeke":

Delightfully, there are some who dare to challenge the idea of quality time. I'm thinking of a situation I experienced on the street, where I stood, as the "adult" child, which I am, and looked at all the interesting figures in a toy shop window. Beside me stood a small boy of 5 or 6; he wanted his father to join with him to look at the dinosaurs. So there he stood!
But no, there wasn't time, because the boy's mother had planned "quality time" so now she grabbed the rest of the family and hurried them because they had to go home and have buns and cocoa. The boy was numbingly indifferent to the offer of "quality time" with the cocoa treat. He just stood and stared at the dinosaurs!

But when the day is planned right down to the smallest detail for optimal use of every second, so the mother can tell her friends about all the things she has done with her children on weekends, there's no alternative. There is no time for dinosaurs and other ancient creatures!

~

I can't help thinking - *Where* is the enjoyment in all this - in this family's togetherness?
How many people live their lives according to what they believe other people might think, and strive for things to appear fine and proper on the outside!

I myself have been one of the biggest sinners within the "field of enjoyment." I was never present mentally, wherever I was ... I was with my children, my husband, but I just *wasn't* there! I could not *enjoy* – could not just be there and enjoy the precious moments, because mentally I was elsewhere!

I remember one of the first times where I succeeded, after hard and intense work to change my way of being and thinking, where I was asked to step in and take my sleeping son in my arms.

Although of course I, as a mother of three, had been sitting with my children in my arms many times, this was as though it was the first time I *really* was there! I just sat there, felt, smelled *and enjoyed* him and the moment.

Tears just ran down my cheeks – both of joy but also of sadness at all the things that I had missed out on throughout the years. I always had something I *just* had to fix or take care of *before* I could allow myself to enjoy! But that moment never came; I was never finished and ready to enjoy!

Allow love to fill your life! But be aware – it does not come by itself!

It is a decision to be taken and you have to work for it!

Life is so short and our children grow up so fast – time flies and will never come again!
Life must be lived, as if every day was your last – live it to the full. Live *and enjoy*!

What are *you* waiting for?

IT IS YOUR LIFE; SEIZE IT, CREATE IT, ENJOY IT ... AND LOVE!

~

LIFE IS A GAME AND THE GAME IS LIFE!

Frank Gormsen

Personal notes and comments:

Chapter 15

WHOSE LIFE ARE YOU LIVING?
FOR *WHOSE* SAKE DO YOU DO THE THINGS YOU DO?

Are your initial thoughts and your sharp retort: *My* life of course! For *my* sake! Then just stop and think about your life once more. Really think!

Try and reflect on some of your daily situations, for example, at home, at work, and at leisure, and try also to reflect on some of your relationships, your contact and the time spent with your parents, your husband/wife/partner, your children, your colleagues, etc.

Why do you do what you do, say what you say, and think what you think?

If you still respond with the same clear and resonant voice and without the slightest doubt in your mind: *For **my** sake!*, then you're among the very few. It's only about 3% of people who have *learned* to live their own lives - *for* their own sake and *based on* their own life values and goals!

If you, as one of the very few, have managed to create *your* life and now live it as you wish, then you've come very far – yes, much farther than most: you earn what *you* want to earn (or you are on your way to it), you have your clear goals for yourself and for your life, your work and your income, for your relationships with friends, partners, children, etc. You have found the inner peace and strength that lies in knowing what *you* want, what *you* can do, and *who* you are! You know that *everything* you do and pursue in life is for your own sake and not either *for* others or to *gain* others' approval, admiration or recognition! The vast majority allow themselves and their lives to be totally or partially controlled by others or by outside influences!

The fact that we let ourselves and our dreams be steered or hindered by what we *believe* others expect of us or what we *believe* they think, has become such an established and ingrained part of our lives and our thought patterns that we do not even question it anymore!

The "mournful" scenario is when a person is not even aware of it, or even worse, is aware but still *allows* it to happen and continue!

Everything we do and say (or don't do and say) has implications for our own lives and the relationships we are in or have with others for everything we think is reflected in our behaviour and thus in the results we achieve. We choose, for example, whether we will react to or act in a particular incident, and that will in turn influence what will happen in our lives. It will affect *everything*, both large and small!

You may know them from your own life, or you've certainly seen or heard about them from others, the ones commonly known as the "dream stealers"! (*See Chapter 2*)

They are those who, mostly out of sheer love and concern for you and for your welfare, manage to steal or crush all your dreams and hopes for a different, and better, life!

Those people appear to have all the possible and impossible reasons for precisely why *you* cannot, may not, or should not!

Whether we like it or not, our relationships to others *will* change when and if we change just as our lives will be affected, or changed, if any of those whom we are surrounded by, or are related to, change. We simply can't avoid this.

The only thing we *can* and *must* deal with is *whether* (and if so, how much) we'll let it affect us, and our way of life!
We *choose* whether or how we will act or react on what's happening in our lives!

Should others' reactions, attitudes or opinions limit or enrich our lives?
Should others' life values and attitudes, based naturally on their own disappointments, defeats, bitterness and restrictions, stop and prevent you from living *your* life?

In my years as a self-employed person I have often seen people to be inspired by a dream, a hope, that they too could change their lives. They stand with one of those unique opportunities and with everything they need to live their dreams and possibly make the career change they have always dreamed of, but still they allow themselves to be stopped by negative partners, parents, friends, etc.

In such situations only one of two things can happen! Either they are so strong-willed, believe so much in themselves and have such big goals and desires for a different and new life, that they continue, *in spite of* all the "worried" or negative people in their lives, and then, inevitably the negative relationships they are in will be abandoned for something better.

Or, they let the "dream stealers" win and they back out! They let themselves be convinced that they can't, that it is definitely not something for them, and that they'd *never* have success with it anyway!

By letting the "dream stealers" win, by accepting the others' views and attitudes, they must resign themselves to the fact, and wave goodbye to their own hopes and dreams!

I have, as I mentioned earlier, seen many who have stood with a unique opportunity, and watched them sense new opportunities for themselves and their future. I had seen a light and a hope ignited in them, but after a while they once again allowed themselves to be persuaded and convinced that *they* could not, or that the possibility was not the right thing, and then abandoned their ideas and dreams completely and return to live the life they lived before!

But now they are filled with even more frustration and even resentment, both towards those who stopped them, but perhaps just as much towards themselves, for having *allowed* themselves to be stopped!

How do *you* feel about yourself if you have given in to others' opinions or dropped something, you really fervently burned for, because you, there on the threshold of something new and unknown, became scared and unsure or let yourself be convinced about something else?

You probably became frustrated, angry, confused, sad and resigned?

What now? Can you forgive yourself, can you forgive others?

If we choose to give up and resign, the emotions and disappointments, both towards the others and also towards yourself, will be strong in the beginning, but they will decrease over time as we convince ourselves that the others were right!

The pain in the chest, the anger, the loss and frustration will be reduced and tucked away, until eventually, after weeks, months, years, they will finally be forgotten and life will go on the same as before.

For such *is* life after all! We go: *That's how it was for my grandparents, my parents and of course for me. Life IS tough and unfair!*

It's actually more than likely that one day when they see someone, who is very close to them, pursuing their own dreams, even they may be among those who oppose and object, probably unconsciously thinking: *If I couldn't, they shouldn't be allowed to either!*

It's not a new phenomenon that those who were bullied or beaten are those who bully or beat others!

If you have ever tried to shut off emotions, had to suppress them because they or you just did not "fit in", then you have probably also experienced that in order to keep them away or down, you have to keep a firm "lid" on them!

We feel perhaps for a period that things go well now that they are hidden away, and we can't feel the pain anymore. Then we can forget them, or so we think!

But there is simply only so much space "inside" and if we time and again must stifle things – the emotions, disappointments and pain – there is a high probability that the "bubble" will eventually burst or that we'll have to dampen the pain, and fill more and more on top of it, so that in the end we almost become like robots!

We cope with each day by kidding ourselves into thinking that this *is* life, a depressing routine without much emotion, without hope for a different or better future.

We all have different ways to stifle things. Many choose, for example food, to physically and mentally put "a lid" on by eating, to fill themselves up with something nice to suppress or to dampen the pain!

Others choose to soothe and drown their sorrows and pain with pills or alcohol. Anything to try and forget, and not to feel reality, not to feel life!

Like Holberg in his classic *"Jeppe on the Mountain" ("Jeppe på Bjerget")*, you may ask: *Why does Jeppe drink?*

As to *your* life:

Why do *you* eat so/too much (and of the wrong things)?

Why do *you* drink too much?

Why do *you* need "happy pills"?

It is *obvious* that you are unable to feel anything and that you feel down-trodden! How can any emotions or feelings penetrate that thick armour you have surrounded yourself with for protection, and that just gets thicker and thicker over the years?

When you store away or try to hold down or suppress, you automatically also keep everything else OUT! It is not possible to let life in because the door has slammed shut!

You do this to avoid being hurt even more/anymore, to protect yourself. With the pain or suffering you previously have experienced, it is easy to convince yourself that you are correct and that it's the right thing to do.

I often hear people say: *Now you don't want to wish for too much – don't aim too high – you could get hurt or disappointed!*

Then it is, according to them, much better and safer to stay away from even trying, or wishing for something new, and eventually even the dreams and hopes that it can be different, begin to disperse because even the dreams can be too painful, and really seem quite impossible with the life you live and the opportunities you *choose to believe* you have!

What *is* this nonsense, to believe that life *must* be tough and it *must* be lived in this way?

Isn't this once again the, *what will the others think* scenario "kicking in"?
Must we avoid going after what we really dream about, just because we risk being hurt, experience challenges, or we might even fail?

Because once our dreams die, what is there left to live and fight for?

You've probably heard this idiom: *It is dangerous to live – you can die from it!*
Death *is* the only certain thing in life! When and how it occurs, we are (thankfully) spared from knowing.
But again and perhaps *precisely* for this very reason, don't we owe it to ourselves to *live* while we can?

Steve Jobs said it so powerful: *Remembering that you are going to die is the best way I know to avoid the trap of thinking you have something to lose. You are already naked. There is no reason not to follow your heart.*

I have personally lived most of my life surrounded by thick and high walls, to keep the painful things out – things which I thought could and would hurt me! I had closed out my feelings and hid them well away so much so that I actually could not feel anything!

I thought, like so many others, that I was safe and secure in this way. I have, to my chagrin, since then learned that I was actually far more vulnerable than I am now, where I have chosen to let go and let life in, with *all* that it entails in terms of challenges, contentment, sorrow, happiness and love!

For the first time in my life, I feel that *I'm* alive – fully and completely!

This personal development I've been through has helped me and taught me that I can stand even stronger than I ever thought possible, now that I'm standing up for myself and know what I want and what I can!

When I step out into the world – into life – with the words: *Here I am, and I stand up for myself,* then there is nothing that can threaten me, because when we are honest and stand up for ourselves, when we take responsibility for all our actions, no one will be able to blackmail us for something we have done or said!

This is not to say that I am never nervous, or never may become frightened and insecure in new situations because just like *everyone* else, I also feel that way when I face something new or dramatic in my life!

But the difference today is that I do not allow it to hinder me! I see it, as Lisa Jimenez refers to it, as my *green light to go*!

Today I know it just indicates that I possess something enormous and that there is a new and exciting learning process ahead of me. It is an opportunity to learn even more and to continue to grow and develop myself.

Bob Proctor says: *Your goal is not big enough, if it doesn't both frighten and excite you at the same time!*

Learn to believe in yourself and what *you* want. Set yourself big goals and go after them – frightened or not – just as long as you do it! (*See Chapter 12*)
There is no development or growth in it for you as a person if the target is too meagre and too easily attainable, if you, for example, already know how to achieve it!

Any person who selects a goal in life which can be fully achieved has already defined his own limitations. – Cavett Robert.

When you take responsibility for your own life, it of course follows that you take responsibility for *all* your actions, the good ones as well as the less fortunate ones, and the day you take that decision, you will be *free*!

It sounds so easy and simple – and it *is*!

It's entirely about taking the decision to do it and then acting on it!

It is simple and straightforward things you have to do, but in practice they are some of the hardest to maintain! Therefore, it is these three qualities, *courage, strength and perseverance*, that characterize those who succeed and these qualities are something *everyone* either has or can learn!

All changes, even those for the better, will create a state of anxiety and trepidation! Your subconscious will fight against everything new, even if that will make your life so much better, and you much happier!

If you don't always have your goal in mind and aren't *constantly* aware of your thoughts and always remind yourself of why you do what you do and what you're aiming for, then all the old thoughts and behavioural patterns will take over so quickly and as easily as the waves washing over the beach pushing all the sand you just dug up, back down into the hole again!

If you are *not* aware of what and how you think, you will then fill your "new life" (your new objective) up faster than you ever thought possible with all the old thoughts and patterns you have just removed and filed away, and before you know it, it's the old and familiar voices that have taken over again! Believe me; they come creeping like a thief in the night!

This is perhaps also why so few, only about 3%, really go all the way, and have achieved the most amazing life with abundance at all levels of their lives!

It is also one of the reasons why you are always advised to find an "accountability partner", a mentor or a tutor – one who has been through the process (and not just read about it in a book or attended a weekend course, and now thinks he/she is ready to save the world)!

That must be someone who from his/her own experience and own heart knows what you're going to go through and who can keep you accountable and on track even when you lose heart and get the urge to give up the struggle and capitulate when the challenges become too arduous.

These struggles make you think only about all the good things and experiences, and the old times are now only remembered as being easy and not complicated!

Then all the familiar words appear: *It wasn't THAT bad! It isn't too bad anyway! There are surely many others who have it even worse than I do! I'll never manage this anyway! This is just not for me, etc.*

So if you are not held accountable and directed back on track, you will end up where you were before, perhaps with the sole exception that now, somewhere there lies a smouldering frustration about being a defeatist!

This feeling can grow even larger over the years; therefore, as I mentioned before, you will find the need to bury it even deeper – put a "lid on it" and dampen the pain!

It is clear that the select little group that actually go all the way will experience public mockery for how should all the others who gave up otherwise bear to see themselves in the mirror every night?

WHAT is easiest to say: *I gave up! I didn't have the belief, courage, strength and perseverance to go after my dreams and goals!* OR: *Ha, look at them; they think they are something special! I'd rather be happy than rich! They are the ones who are causing all the distress and imbalance here on earth! Poor little me, I'm just a "victim"! It's not my fault, it's the others'!*

Of course it is the last version which is the easiest to think and say. It comes most naturally to all those who gave up the belief and the hope that things could become different, and *that* too maybe even after only one single attempt; or to those who have never even tried, and who definitely don't *believe* that it can be different, and certainly that *they* can't have any influence on what, and why things happen, as they do!

Try again to think about this chapter's heading: *WHOSE life are you living? For WHOSE sake do you do the things you do?*

If you shouldn't live *your* life, whilst you're alive, then when should you? *You* are and will be the only one that can allow others and their attitudes and beliefs to control your life, and at worst take your dreams and hopes away from you!

Believe in yourself and never, ever give up even if that means you need to borrow someone else's belief in you for some time, or someone else's eyes, to see the opportunities that are available for you!

We should all remind ourselves of something cyclist Lance Armstrong expressed so clearly in this sentence: *Pain is temporary! Quitting last forever!* Or what General Douglas MacArthur once said: *Age wrinkles the body! Quitting wrinkles the soul!*

Life, love and the most amazing opportunities are simply lying at your feet just waiting for you to gather them up!

Let go of everything that has held you back and kept you down!

Smash down the wall that you believed was a protection, but which in reality is a straitjacket, a straitjacket that prevents you from being able to greet and feel life fully and completely!

Believe in yourself, let go and throw yourself into life! It *is* just a decision!

~

Inspired by Piet Hein *(To risk is to live, to live is to risk!)* Frank Gormsen wrote to me:

If you don't risk, you risk not living. Risking nothing in your life due to the anxiety that you might get hurt, you risk never living. For if you live a life where you do not push the limits, you will never find out just how much you have within you and how much you can actually achieve!

Risk being hurt, risk feeling pain and risk to love unconditionally! Only then can you really achieve feeling life.

Live life with the risk of making mistakes and live life with the risk of achieving what you want!

You only get what you want by taking risks!

~

Personal notes and comments:

CHAPTER 16

I HAVE ALL THAT I WANT IN MY LIFE!

WOW! What an amazing feeling it is, to be able to write these words!

I was completely overwhelmed and tears welled up when I realized what it was I had just written!

I HAVE all that I want in my life! I tell you, I truly do!

But this has definitely not always been the case. Just think that I had to reach my mid-forties before I could say this!

The preceding years have been very intensive and at times very tough and challenging. But although there still remains much work ahead, because I have decided that I *will* continue to develop my amazing life and, therefore, *deliberately* seek the challenges that can help me grow even more as a person, I am convinced today that it is and has been entirely worthwhile!

I recall a lecturer I once heard, who with a big smile said: *It took me 10 years to become an "overnight success"!* It is because it all starts with you taking the decision to change your life, if that's what you want!

Initially the decision, then the first step! So you are well on the way and already you are a success just by taking the decision!

I have for far too many years personally struggled to get everything in order, *before* I believed that I could consider myself a success. I've lived my life on an eternal quest to get the "perfect life". I sought high and low and certainly didn't see what was right under my nose and closest to my heart!

I *have* the most amazing husband, whom I love more than anything and I *have* the three most fantastic children I could wish for! My love for them all is indescribable!

We *have* the most amazing relationship that just gets better and better with time, growing deeper and more expansive! Imagine being *so* privileged as to be in a relationship that just keeps getting better year after year, to be able to see and feel the love grow and develop. I am so deeply grateful for my life!

What is the difference between my life now and my life just a few years ago when I had the same husband, the same children, but was not able to feel and enjoy life? Opposed to today, where I can sit with tears of joy and gratitude in my eyes and say: *I HAVE all that I want in my life!*

The greatest difference is that *I'm present*, in my entirety, and not just in my physical presence! I have re-evaluated my life values and I've found love for myself!

It is impossible to love others if you do not love yourself and for many years, my quest for the "perfect life" was based on all the external, material things and on what I could do and show.

I measured others as I was measured (or more correctly – I *let* myself be measured) based on what you could do, make and owned. I lived by the dictum that you can't be totally content and pleased if you do not have..., can... or do...!

I was caught in the "rat race" and lived, like so many others, solely on external values and in relation to external circumstances!

In my head I was convinced that I could only be happy once I had reached *all* my goals!

Here I'm not referring to all the personal goals or values! I resolutely believed that one's success was measured solely on the basis of whether you reached your goal and not before!

Money was the ultimate factor as to whether you lived a good and happy life, or a poor and miserable one! My understanding was that you were unable to be happy and feel good if you had no money for a lifestyle of largess.

Far too many live as I did, by the dictum: *Show me first – THEN I'll believe it!*

How they mocked me, especially those who were closest to me, when I talked about the dreams and goals I was pursuing and the life that I would get to live!
Ha, ha! Yes of course! WHERE is it then? SHOW it to us! You do not have it in you! You'll never achieve that! What makes you believe that you will ever have or be able to afford that? Be realistic!

In other words: I was not a success in their eyes!

For many years I had let myself be influenced by what (I thought) others thought and envisaged about when I was a success. I strove after all the external and the material things that would *prove* my success, everything that I thought would make me a happy person!

Dale Carnegie said it very well: *It isn't what you have, or who you are, or where you are, or what you are doing that makes you happy or unhappy. It is what you think about!*

I often reflect back to when I as a young woman was sitting alone in my little apartment, which I had furnished bright, white and austere, completely with the "right" things. I sat there alone looking at my almost perfect home, but could not feel myself, I could not feel that I was alive!

It was probably one of the first times I really thought: *There is something wrong with all this! I have what I need, but I do not know WHO I am and WHAT I want, I can't feel anything!* This helplessness and desperation caused me to inflict pain on myself so that I could feel again; that's how emotionally paralysed I had become!

That was my way of reacting. But there are many others who live just as "dead" lives. We all react differently to it! But one common factor is that we do not feel that we are alive!

There are some who choose alcohol or some other euphoriant, many people use food to keep "a lid on", and many choose "happy pills" because otherwise they go around feeling depressed and are missing the contentment and happiness in their otherwise so "perfect" lives! (*See Chapter 15*)

Many can't understand why they have this sadness and numbness, because when they look around, they have everything that should make them happy and content – a loving family, lovely children, a great place to live, the things needed for the house and garden, a good job, the capacity of travelling once in a while to the places of their dreams, etc.

All the exterior stuff is just by the book, then why this sadness, this feeling of not really being present, or not feeling alive?

The more time that passes, the more frustrating things get! The children get bigger, and maybe when they are ready to leave home you suddenly realize that you really haven't been there for them!

Suddenly, you stand there thinking: *Where did the time go? What happens now when the kids are leaving? What are my responsibilities now? Who is this husband/wife I'm sitting here with? How is our relationship really and what do we have in common now? Is this the life I really want? Why am I not happy? There must be something wrong with me! Doctor, Doctor! Give me some medicine so that I can be happy and feel something again!*

What kind of life is this that so many *choose* to live?
We believe it should be this way! We've seen it with our parents, grandparents, friends, etc.
Many marriages end in divorce, because they grow unhappy with it. It didn't give them what they once thought it would give them. The life they aspired to, their ideal vision, their dream life, everything turned out to be quite different in reality. What went wrong?

We may begin in a small way, to do or buy different things to feel contented again. We buy dreams! But it *is* like peeing in your pants to keep warm!

We revel in magazines – other people's dreams, crises, disasters!

It is almost like, *the worse news the better* for it helps to put our own, probably a little less chaotic, lives into perspective and we can continue a little longer because our lives are probably not quite so bad after all!

Another "advantage" of keeping the focus on others' tragedies and accidents is that we do not need to relate to our own! Many actually use the fact that they must take care of everybody else's problems (that of family or friends) as an excuse for not dealing with or doing something about their own lives.

When we whine and complain, we end up in a self-created "victim role" and thereby we disclaim any responsibility and thus also every opportunity to change our lives!

It *is* difficult to accept that you are responsible for your life as it is today and how it's going to be in the future.

This has been said and written before, but it can't be repeated often enough: *If you continue to have the thoughts you've always had and you continue to do what you've always done, you will continue to have and get what you have always got!*

Many go on their dream vacation once in a while. It's actually something that many have been planning and saving up for, for a long time. Many are trying to flee their daily lives, their reality, to feel the rush, to feel that they are alive and to enjoy the luxury far away from the daily grind. They can live high on the memories for some time, but almost at once they get the longing to escape from the boring everyday life again as soon as possible! It becomes like a drug for them, something they need to "survive" their tough and maybe dismal life.

For many families it is the highlight of the year and holidays are planned and prepared down to the minutest details. However, it is all too often funded with borrowed money, so they will have to work even harder when they come home, to pay back the loan! Then they become even wearier of their lives, which they now believe to be both harsher and even more unjust. You hear them say: *I've got to get away again, otherwise I will not survive!*

Imagine spending just as much time in planning our lives!

Suppose we began to set some goals for our lives and our daily routine and then began to work for it, just the same way we do in planning a short getaway!

What if you don't get to go on your holiday for one or several years – a holiday where everything is used up anyway after a week or two and where you must scrimp and borrow again to get the next "fix"?

If instead you plan your life and follow it carefully, it will soon give you all the possibilities, all the prosperity, happiness, contentment and love that you dream about!

Why aren't more people planning their own lives instead of just planning their short vacation? It's probably because they find it hard to *believe* that they can change anything, or that it can ever be any different!

There is no place where we learn how to set goals and learn to take responsibility for our own lives and happiness! We don't learn it in school; we don't learn it from our family or our friends and acquaintances.

Even those who are really trying, those who really want to change something in their lives and decide to do something about it, will often stop at the first challenge they face, and then the ingrained thoughts return once again; *Phew! It's not easy; it's probably not something for me anyway! I can't do it!*

Then doubts start to fester!

It doesn't require as much planning to go for a week's holiday, than it requires going for a better and more prosperous life forever!

One thing is that we do not *believe* that we can; we do not believe that it *is* for us to achieve! Another thing is that we either do not understand what it takes, or if we do, we do not persevere enough in our work with ourselves and our personal development. It obviously requires a lot to achieve your goal, to change things in your life that you're not satisfied with! It is so much more than just changing the exterior: for example, finding a new partner, moving, having a child, finding a new job!

It is yourself, your thoughts and behavioural patterns, and not least your vision of yourself, which needs to be changed *and kept changed!*

Changing it is one of the most essential requirements to achieve what you want in your life! It can be really challenging to change and go against your usual thoughts for it requires constant attention!

But the day you sit there and are able to say *I have all that I want in my life,* then you will know that it *is* all worthwhile!

Imagine a life where *every* day you live your dream, instead of having to resort to a "fix" every now and again just to keep your life going!
Then all the exterior things, all the things that money can buy, will be the "icing on the cake"! *Of course* it's also worthwhile going after the "icing on the cake" – all the things that can fill our lives and everyday with even more colour, contentment and pleasure!

But we have become a society of "poor victims" where it's *everyone else's fault!*

We are full of explanations and excuses about why we can't, are not allowed to, and do not deserve.

We do not accept any responsibility for our own lives usually because we don't *know* we have the possibility to change it ourselves, or sometimes because it hurts too much to realize that we ourselves are responsible for where we stand today and for the lives we live!

Therefore, we fill ourselves with "happy pills", "put the lid on", turn a blind eye to things, revel at other people's misfortunes, and engross ourselves in soap-operas and inane television series! We buy ourselves a little short-lived contentment – new furniture, a new house, a new car (cars) – or we go on a "dream trip" and then live on the memories, which in all probability are so far from our dismal and stressful day!

We feel like prisoners in our own lives, like spectators to the life that passes us by!

We often ponder: *One day I will...! THEN things will be completely different! I JUST need to finish my education! When the children have left home, JUST you wait and see!* All of these remain dreams because they never became concrete targets, and there was never any comprehensive plan to go after them.

Many reach a point where it is the weekly lottery tickets that keep their dreams alive. Many people spend many pounds every week on *What if...? Wow! THEN I can...!*
Imagine if people, instead, chose to spend their money on themselves and their personal development, and began to consciously work towards creating their dream life, how great could be the results?

Russell Conwell's classic *"Acres of Diamonds"* describes how a person sells his home and his land to go and look for gold and diamonds, only to die poor and lonely years later in a deserted and remote location.

The story continues that the man, who purchased his land, found one of the largest diamond mines ever on the very same ground that the man had sold him!

Isn't that what most of us do, just in a figurative sense?

In our attempts or eagerness to "fix" the things in our lives, we are unhappy with or we feel we are missing, for example, happiness, love and better self-esteem, we go looking for the answer and the solution outside of ourselves. We look to a partner, a friend, a child or a parent to fill the void. Perhaps we expect that a new job, new house, a child/another child will satisfy our "hunger"!

But, as in Russell Conwell's story, our search outside ourselves will leave us empty-handed and "poor", while if we dig deep into our own "garden" and search inward, then we might find all the gold and the diamonds we could wish for!

James Allen wrote: *Only by much searching and mining are gold and diamonds obtained and a person can find every truth connected with his being, if he will dig deep into the mind of his soul.*

Jim Rohn wrote: *The greatest source of unhappiness comes from within.*

It is in fact there, and *only* there, that the source of true contentment resides!

So, instead of searching outside or far away, spend some time EACH DAY to look inward! Instead of expecting that something or someone will come from outside to "fill you up" and make you content, you must learn to do the "filling-up" yourself!

Take the decision that you will grow, that you will find your way to your true values.
Decide to do whatever it takes so that you too can one day say;
I HAVE all that I want in my life!

With these fundamental elements in order, then there is something to build on – something that is stable and solid, not just dreams and castles in the air. It is very difficult to stack enough lottery tickets, travel magazines and vacation pictures together to form an equally stable and solid foundation for *your* life!

Love and especially your inner strength and serenity *are* the key building blocks for a happy, fuller and richer life! Everything else is the "icing on the cake" that just makes it even more amazing! It's not just a short pleasure or a "quick fix" – It's *every day*, you can choose to feel good and feel that you're alive!

Well, it was long ago and so much has happened since I sat there alone in my little apartment until today, when the tears once again run down my cheeks, but now out of sheer gratitude for being able to write: *I HAVE all that I want in my life!*

Even more amazing is the knowledge that I have only just begun to explore and *live* my life!

There is now the awareness that life is just lying there at my feet, the definite knowledge that *everything* is possible, that I can get everything I want and wish for in my life!

But I already *have* the most important component of them all! I have LOVE – love for myself, my husband and my children – and I am loved back!

*I HAVE FOUND **MY** "DIAMOND MINE"!*

Personal notes and comments:

Chapter 17

WHAT HAS YOUR UPBRINGING MEANT FOR YOU?

My name comes from the Latin *Benedict* and means "the blessed" – and *that* I am!

I was destined for something great, created to make a big difference in many people's lives! My creator created me and all the other people on this earth as the most perfect creatures, with all the abilities, qualities, attributes and qualifications needed to live the most amazing life, a life filled to the brim with abundance on all levels!

I've been given the strength and courage to face the adversities that arise and which must be faced and I have, through my personal development, learned that the *less* I fight against, the easier it becomes!
It's when you fight against that which *should* be and that which *should* happen, that life becomes difficult!

I've accepted that sometimes I *am* in deep water and that it is precisely only by throwing myself into the deep and unknown waters that I can progress in life! *This* creates the development required for me to take the next step and progress with my amazing life!

I will help many and I will come to influence many through my being, and through what I share and do here on Earth! I was created for something big and the paths to where I am today have been filled with challenges, but it's all the challenges that have made me into who I am today!

God gives us no greater challenges than God knows we can handle - so it is said.

God must therefore have great confidence in me. I am grateful that God shows this confidence in me!

I am only now beginning to see and understand *how huge* life is! How amazing life is when you allow it in, let go and stop fighting, but observe and explore with curiosity, openness and enthusiasm!

It's not something you can learn from a book, for words alone make no sense, they awaken no echo in the heart! Words are words and they are thought! Life, however, must be experienced and lived with *all* the senses and emotions!

Just like Don Quixote fighting the windmills, most of us are fighting the demons in our lives!

But these demons are *they* real. Or are they only in our thoughts? Is it the memories and experiences from the past which persecute us?

Then, is it not up to us alone to decide just how much influence these demons should have on us and how much they should control our lives?

Don't we all have "skeletons in our closets", things and experiences that we carry around from our past, including those from our childhood, from the small (which from the outside may seem as fairly harmless experiences), to the more menacing ones like abuse, rage, etc.

Even those completely innocent things that were only said in fun – for example, nicknames, name games – may have stuck and unconsciously have been perceived as being the truth about ourselves, our appearance or our abilities; a "reality" and truth, we now live our lives by and which we allow to control our lives! (*See Chapter 5*)

They may well have sunk in and stuck and they can still affect our thinking and behavioural patterns even long after the actual "experiences" or incidents.

Many experience that it is the *anxiety*, that it might/will happen again, that controls their lives, on a subconscious level.

The experiences, memories, and the people who were involved, have become the demons in our thoughts and in our hearts and as long as we fight to keep them away, anxious that they may return and "it" will happen again, we will keep life at bay! We fear the past and what has happened! Anxiety and fear have taken over far too many and it is this anxiety that today governs their thought and behavioural patterns and thus their lives!

But try to read what Tom Payne says: *We can't fear the past. Fear is a future thing. Since the future is all in our heads, fear must be a "head thing."*

If you really can understand and take this in, you will be free; free to move forward and let go of the past. Free to LIVE!

It is precisely this letting go that it's all about for the energy you spend on holding on to the past is so draining and tiring that it can prevent you from living richly and fully!

Mary Manin Morrissey wrote it this way: *Even though you might want to have momentum in your life, then it can be that you actually have one foot on the brake! To be free we must learn how to let go! Slip the pain free! Release the fear! Refuse to cooperate with your old pain! The energy you use to hold onto the past is holding you back from a new life!*

I have lived with many demons, anxiety and a sense of insecurity, which was founded way back during my childhood!

When you're a young child, you don't always understand what happens, or why things happen as they do, and you can't always extract the significance along the way!

An experience that is burdened with guilt and shame in a child's head, if not corrected by an adult, will result in the child taking the responsibility for the situation upon itself, and creating all sorts of possible, or rather impossible, thoughts and feelings about itself and its own self worth!

A child is like an open book, and everything it is told, all the words and experiences it is "fed" – both good and bad – will be seen and believed by the child to be the truth and made to be its own!

These words and experiences will therefore affect the child's self-image, its thoughts and behavioural patterns and these will follow it throughout its live – unless later in life it learns and understands the processes or mechanisms I talk about in this book, and *chooses* to take responsibility for its own life, simply by changing its thoughts and behavioural patterns!

Similarly with my own process and development, what has been one of the greatest experiences, one of the biggest breakthroughs and most overwhelming insight I have had was when I finally realized that I for many years had allowed myself, my life, and my relationships with others to be steered by a frightened, anxious and guilt-ridden little girl (in *my* adult body)!

But how can you possibly explain this to others who have not experienced something similar, who have not been through the same processes?
How do you, for example, explain or describe a tree, or colours, to a blind person?

It is equally impossible!

If I were to describe how I lived, it would be like a little girl in a grown woman's body. The adult body was like a shell or a cocoon with holes for eyes, and inside sat this little scared girl looking terrified out at the world! *Nothing* that she saw or experienced fitted into her little world, or was in harmony with her thoughts or self-awareness!

The body she was in did not fit. She could not relate to what she saw in the mirror. The body, as *she* saw it, was big and shapeless!

Nothing of what she saw or experienced, she could understand or relate to, and, therefore, she became even more confused and uncertain, which further resulted in only more anxiety in her mind!

If you, for example, are not aware that it is a scared and insecure 4-year-old who is steering and controlling your life, many thoughts and behavioural patterns may be very difficult to understand – not only for oneself but also for others!

Think, for example, just how the relationship to, and interaction with, other adults might be!

Try to think of the following:

- *What has your upbringing meant for you?*

- *What are your usual or fixed thoughts and behavioural patterns, and when were they founded?*

- *Who or what controls your life?*

- *Who is it who act and react when you face new and challenging situations?*

Have you ever considered that there is always a reason for the way you or others react, and that it is *never* as a result of the actual incident – but it is *always* based on what you or the other person have previously experienced, and are now carrying around as "excess luggage"?

If you think about how few actually possess this insight, then it's actually no wonder that we so often misunderstand each other!

This is primarily because we always act and react based on what we have experienced and accepted, and what we have converted into our way of thinking, acting and living!

Everything in life is a choice and a "struggle". You always have to make choices and understand that all your thoughts and actions *do have* consequences! We must understand the importance of accepting and facing these struggles and challenges! Understand and accept that they never end if we want to grow and develop as people, because if we do not participate, or throw ourselves into these struggles and into life by accepting the challenges as they arrive, we will just fall asleep! We will become numb! Then life will pass us by! We will just watch it go by – and do nothing! Days turn into month and month turn into years.

Therefore, knowledge of where you stand now; what and why you think and act like you do, and not least a clear picture of what you want to achieve, is so essential for you reaching your goals.

Take responsibility for yourself, your personal development and your life! Decide that it will be *YOU* who is at the helm!

YOUR LIFE IS YOUR RESPONSIBILITY!

Personal notes and comments:

Personal notes and comments:

THANK YOU

Now that you have read this book, I am sure there is someone whom you know and love, who might also need and benefit from reading it.

I therefore urge you to spread the knowledge of my book by referring to this link: **http://www.amazon.com/dp/B009K7S2L8**

Please help me by giving your own testimonial on Amazon or send a mail to: info@personligsucces.nu

- Thanking you in advance

Benedicte Frölich

ABOUT THE AUTHOR

Benedicte Frölich was born in Denmark in 1964.
She is the mother of three, trained nurse and Expressive Art
Therapist and she has more than 20 years of experience as an
entrepreneur in the NM industry

Since 1994 Benedicte has studied and worked with some of the
greatest names in the Personal Development industry -
including Jim Rohn , Brian Tracy, Bob Proctor, Zig Ziglar and
many more - all talking and writing about the most basic
knowledge; " You are and get what you think" and "Your
thoughts affect your emotions and feelings, your feelings affect
your actions and your actions affect your results - and thus
your life! "
A very intensive course, for more than seven years (and
ongoing), with her two personal mentors, has resulted in what
she today personally describes as; *"The most abundant life on
all levels ! A life where I live by my own values and experience the
inner peace that comes when you stand up for yourselves, know
who you are, what you stand for and what you can and want in
your life."*

Benedicte Frölich's book *"The Key to a Rich Life - Thoughts are
like seeds ... You reap what you sow"* has quickly become a
bestseller both in Denmark and abroad, and has received wide
recognition and fantastic reviews from some of the biggest
names both nationally and internationally include Brian Tracy,
Vic Johnson, Kyle Wilson and many more.

Moreover, Benedicte, as one of the few in the world – with her focus and persistence for more than three years – has got none other than Bob Proctor to not just to read her book but actually choosing to write the foreword to it!

Benedicte Frölich´s books are all based on her own personal progress and experience and the knowledge she has acquired over the many years of study.

Benedicte has worked as an independent author, mentor and speaker together with her husband Frank Gormsen since '97. Together they hold courses, lectures and training sessions for larger and smaller groups of individuals and other independent contractors. She is also co-creator and co-owner of a Web.TV Chanel about Success and Personal Development.

THERE IS A RESPONSIBILITY TO BE TAKEN

- AND A LIFE TO BE LIVED!

Benedicte Frölich

www.ingramcontent.com/pod-product-compliance
Lightning Source LLC
Chambersburg PA
CBHW022007000426
42741CB00007B/923